Fascism: A Very Short Introduction

VERY SHORT INTRODUCTIONS are for anyone wanting a stimulating and accessible way into a new subject. They are written by experts, and have been translated into more than 45 different languages.

The series began in 1995, and now covers a wide variety of topics in every discipline. The VSI library now contains over 500 volumes—a Very Short Introduction to everything from Psychology and Philosophy of Science to American History and Relativity—and continues to grow in every subject area.

Titles in the series include the following:

Kevin Passmore

FASCISM

A Very Short Introduction

OXFORD
UNIVERSITY PRESS

OXFORD
UNIVERSITY PRESS

Great Clarendon Street, Oxford, OX2 6DP,
United Kingdom

Oxford University Press is a department of the University of Oxford.
It furthers the University's objective of excellence in research, scholarship,
and education by publishing worldwide. Oxford is a registered trade mark of
Oxford University Press in the UK and in certain other countries

© Kevin Passmore 2014

The moral rights of the author have been asserted

First published as a Very Short Introduction 2002
Second edition published 2014

Impression: 11

Published in the United States of America by Oxford University Press
198 Madison Avenue, New York, NY 10016, United States of America

British Library Cataloguing in Publication Data
Data available

Library of Congress Control Number: 2014933830

ISBN 978-0-19-968536-3

Printed in Great Britain by
Ashford Colour Press Ltd., Gosport, Hampshire.

Fascism has an enigmatic countenance because in it appears the most counterpoised contents. It asserts authoritarianism and organises rebellion. It fights against contemporary democracy and, on the other hand, does not believe in the restoration of any past rule. It seems to pose itself as the forge of a strong State, and uses means most conducive to its dissolution, as if it were a destructive faction or a secret society. Whichever way we approach fascism we find that it is simultaneously one thing and the contrary, it is A and not A...

José Ortega y Gasset, 'Sobre el Fascismo' (1927)

Contents

Preface to the second edition

Since 2002, when the first edition of *Fascism: A Very Short Introduction* was published, a double shift in method has transformed the field. Then, the objective was to produce an exact definition of fascism (a 'model' or a 'typology'), which would encapsulate its key features. This definition would allow us to identify fascist movements, normally assumed to be national variants of the same 'thing'. Now, scholars doubt the usefulness of a definition of fascism, even if it was possible to agree on one. Instead, they urge us to explore how and why the term was actually used by people in the past and for what purposes. They also doubt that the world can be broken up into national cases, given the enormous fluidity of economies, ideas, and human migrations. Fascism is now being studied as a 'transnational' phenomenon, and we can ask how protagonists transferred the term across national frontiers.

The first edition of *Fascism* reflected my partial awareness of the drawbacks of definitions but in the end, I invoked these problems only to produce one of my own. Consequently, while the chapter structure and some sections of the new edition are unchanged, the argument and much of the content is completely new.

Like the first edition, this book synthesizes an enormous range of scholarship, and it remains impossible to express fully my debt to those upon whose work I have drawn. Of the scholars whose work I singled out for special thanks in the first edition that of Michael Burleigh and Wolfgang Wipperman remains essential. Above all, the new edition bears the imprint of the ideas of the French political scientist Michel Dobry, who has done so much to revise the way that scholars understand and use concepts and categories.

My ideas have been sharpened in early morning discussions over coffee with Hugh Compston. My thanks are due to Garthine Walker, who read the entire manuscript, to the anonymous readers for their incisive comments, and to Emma Ma for her encouraging editorship.

Following convention, I have used 'Fascism' to refer to the Italian movement and regime and 'fascism' to refer to the generic concept.

List of illustrations

List of maps

Chapter 1
'A and not A': what is fascism?

23 March 1919

Only a few dozen men and a handful of women attended the meeting in the hall overlooking the Piazza San Sepolcro in Milan, hitherto remarkable only for its 11th-century church. Benito Mussolini had called the participants together to inaugurate the Fasci di Combattimento (Groups of Fighters), one of the many tiny veteran groups that used the 'fasci' label. The last thing on their minds was the foundation of an ideology, let alone a theoretical definition.

Mussolini, then aged 35, was an ex-socialist and war veteran. This son of a small-town blacksmith had recently been cultivating a more up-market image, shaving off his moustache and wearing collared shirts. Yet his only visible source of income was as editor of a struggling newspaper, *Il Popolo d'Italia (The Italian People)*, which was insufficient to maintain his wife and three children, his mistress, and his liking for fencing, duelling, and fast cars. Already a man who lived from politics, he was acquiring a taste for living in style from politics.

That was unfortunate, for in 1919 Mussolini lacked an obvious place in the political landscape. He had left the Socialist Party because it opposed Italian intervention in the Great War, and he had joined syndicalists (revolutionary trade unionists), nationalists, and elements of the governing Liberals (who were conservative by modern standards) in the pro-war movement. Beyond the question of the war, so-called Interventionists had little in common. Some saw intervention as a way to provoke revolution, though of what sort was unclear. Others claimed that war would regenerate the bourgeoisie or provide popular support for the existing regime. Some simply wished to outmanoeuvre rivals in parliament. During the war, Mussolini's patriotic journalism had been useful to the government because of his supposed influence among workers. Now he was cut off from the socialists, but had not given up hope of recovering his appeal to them; his calls for revolution alienated the right, and he faced competition from more prestigious Interventionist leaders such as the poet Gabriele d'Annunzio. Mussolini and his allies had an obvious interest in perpetuating the wartime spirit and in trading on their status as veterans.

The term 'fasces' potentially possessed the broad appeal that they needed. Literally, it meant a tightly-bound bundle of rods, sometimes used as the handle for an axe. Its first political use, by Sicilian peasant socialists in the 1890s, lent the word an air of popular radicalism that comforted ex-leftists among the Interventionists. It simultaneously appealed to Liberals and nationalists because in ancient Rome it symbolized authority. By 1919, Interventionists monopolized use of the label 'fasci'.

In his Piazza San Sepolcro speech, Mussolini avoided formulating a programme. He merely endorsed that of a nationalist labour union, without agreeing to its specific points—after all, he was meeting in a room lent by a local employers' association. What became known as the '1919 Programme' was drawn up some weeks later. It combined nationalism with republicanism, anticlericalism, women's suffrage, and social reform, much of which Fascists would soon jettison. The Fascists rejected dogmas and ideologies.

Within two years, Fascism had become a mass movement, but it had not clarified its meaning. Its paramilitary formations attacked Socialist and Catholic organizations and Slavic minorities while condemning capitalism. Mussolini lambasted Roman political corruption, yet negotiated a deal with established politicians, thanks to which, on 22 October 1922, he became prime minister at the head of a Fascist-Liberal coalition.

In 1926, Mussolini began to establish a full-scale dictatorship. He made programmatic statements while intellectuals such as Giovanni Gentile systematized Fascist ideas. The regime implemented practical policies. Fascism certainly did not lack ideology, but its nature was never certain. The regime changed with time and activists did not agree on issues from the role of women and trade unions in society, to the relationship between party and state, and the nature of a national literature.

Uncertainty about the meaning of fascism did not prevent it from winning plaudits outside Italy. Fascism was becoming one of the great political movements of the 20th century, and by the 1930s, many people would see the struggle between fascism and antifascism as the primary issue in domestic and international politics. Already in 1925 at least 45 groups in several countries called themselves 'fascist', encouraged to do so by the Italian regime's efforts to spread its influence. Yet these movements were not simple copies. They were no more homogenous than the original; they emphasized some aspects of what they saw in Italy, and ignored or mistook others; they combined Italian with other foreign influences and with their own traditions. Some movements that to our eyes look similar to Fascism rejected the label.

The rise of Nazism in Germany further complicated matters. Hitler had been among the many enthusiasts for Fascism, and Nazism's supporters and enemies sometimes referred to it as 'fascist'. Yet Nazism was as hard to define as Fascism and it included elements, such as radical antisemitism, that had featured much less strongly in Fascism. Hitler's success somewhat eclipsed Mussolini's international reputation; Fascism began to borrow from Nazism and foreign movements shifted their allegiance to the latter, emphasizing antisemitism and 'national socialism'.

After 1945, fascism was discredited, but its legacy continued to structure the political landscape. Governments in Russia, Britain, and North America drew legitimacy from their role in defeating fascism, while the French, Italian, and German regimes claimed descent from the Resistance. 'Fascism' became a term of abuse. Not surprisingly, those who mimic fascism have rarely been politically relevant. In the 1990s, movements emerged that many of their opponents saw as an updating of fascism, but the groups in question nearly always rejected the label.

Definitions and theories of fascism

How can we make sense of an ideology that appeals to skinheads and intellectuals; preaches revolution while allying with conservatives; adopts a macho style yet attracts many women; calls for return to tradition yet is fascinated by technology; idealizes the people yet is contemptuous of mass society, and advocates both violence and order? Fascism, as Ortega y Gasset says, is always 'A and not A'.

The conventional way to cut through these problems is to establish a precise definition (often called a 'model' or a 'typology'). This definition is meant to encapsulate the most important features of fascism and to identify movements as fascist or not, even if they did not use the label themselves. It is deceptively simple to list the characteristics of fascism (see Box 1):

Box 1

A	B
Ultranationalism	Resistance to transcendence (Ernst Nolte)
Charismatic leadership	
Dictatorship	A dictatorship of the most reactionary elements of monopoly capitalism (The Communist International)
Racism	
Antisemitism	
A single party	A political ideology whose mythic core in its various permutations is a palingenetic form of populist ultranationalism (Roger Griffin)
Paramilitarism	
Violence, actual or threatened	A political religion (Emilio Gentile)
Corporatism	
A totalitarian ideology	
Anticapitalism	
Antisocialism and anticommunism	
Antiliberalism	
Antiparliamentarianism	
Anticonstitutionalism	

Column A lists terms that appear frequently in scholarly definitions and that fascists themselves might have recognized. At first sight, they are sufficiently uncontroversial that one might accuse anyone who today advocated three or more of them of displaying 'fascist tendencies'. Yet serious examination reveals problems. Must a movement display all of these features to be fascist, or just some of them? If the answer is 'some', then which ones?

The individual parts of the definition are problematic too. For instance, those who called themselves fascists were not straightforwardly nationalist. Rather they wanted to exclude, imprison, or kill many people who were part of the nation. Mussolini sometimes invoked an international 'universal fascism', while in occupied Europe, collaborators aspired to a place in a German-dominated New Order. In Alsace, Nazi sympathizers advocated regionalism rather than nationalism. It might seem obvious that fascists all wanted dictatorship and one-party rule, but there was much conflict between state and party in the Fascist and Nazi regimes, while some Italian syndicalists wanted a small state. Even when fascists agreed on something, such as corporatism, they could not agree what that involved. And there are obvious differences between Fascism and Nazism regarding antisemitism.

Given these difficulties, some argue that fascism is better-defined in terms of what it opposed. And yet fascists did not all oppose communism, say, for the same reasons. Moreover, they simultaneously endeavoured to learn from it and use its methods. Others argue that a successful definition would do more than merely list features of fascism. They advise us that some aspects are more fundamental than others are, for they explain the causes and dynamic of fascism. That's where the definitions in the right hand column come in—scholarly definitions that protagonists might not have used, and perhaps angrily rejected. Leaving aside for the moment what these definitions mean, note only that there are nearly as many definitions of fascism as there are scholars of fascism and that they do not agree which of them is correct. In my view, the definitional approach suffers from intrinsic flaws.

In the rest of this chapter, I shall review some of the principal ways in which fascism has been defined. Since there are so many ways of doing so, I shall simplify. I shall group theories according to whether they see the conservative or the radical sides of fascism as fundamental. I have done that because it shows that the debate over fascism represents a continuation of the conflicts of the age of fascism itself. In the interwar years, the left saw itself as engaged in a struggle of progressive 'antifascists' against reactionary fascism and its conservative allies, while the moderate right and centre countered that the real conflict was between democrats and revolutionary-totalitarian extremists of left and right. The disadvantage for scholars of continuing these struggles is that the political stakes rigidify the concept of fascism, whereas in practical use it was uncertain and contested. This hardening may cause scholars to mistake their own definition for *the* definition. In fact, we shall see that while each theory tells us *something*, none represents the only way of understanding fascism. In effect, each definition arbitrarily designates some aspects of fascism as primary and others as secondary. I shall conclude the chapter by suggesting an alternative approach.

Marxist approaches

In its simplest form, Marxism assumes that modern society is divided into two fundamental classes: the bourgeoisie, or capitalists, who own the means of production (tools, factories), and the working classes, or proletariat, who do not own the means of production and so must work for wages. Capitalists and proletarians struggle for ownership of the means of production and control over the state. Between these two great classes are the petty bourgeoisie, including self-employed traders, small business, peasants, and white-collar workers. The petty bourgeoisie is uncertain whether to side with capital or labour, for it owns productive property and yet is exploited by big business.

Marxist approaches to fascism all emphasize its links with capitalism and the petty bourgeoisie. The first influential definition was that of the Communist International in 1935, which stated that 'Fascism in power is the open, terroristic dictatorship of the most reactionary, the most chauvinistic and most imperialistic elements of finance capitalism'. The International claimed that as the proletariat's revolutionary sentiment intensified, capitalists would use terror to defend their property.

However, the crisis of capitalism was allegedly so serious that conventional dictatorship was inadequate, and so capitalists used the Fascist movement to destroy socialism. According to the International, this mass movement recruited from the petty bourgeoisie. Although the petty bourgeoisie had real grievances against big capital, Fascists were able to persuade it that its interest lay in defending property against socialism. Once Fascism was in power and the labour movement destroyed, capitalists no longer needed the petty-bourgeois fascist party, and so it was suppressed or marginalized.

Marxists did not unanimously endorse the International's definition. First, in the 1960s and 1970s, some felt that the petty bourgeoisie played a more independent role than the International had allowed, and to some extent opposed capitalist interests. Second, and more recently, some historians have annexed the concept of 'governmentality'. Developed by the great French philosopher-historian, Michel Foucault, governmentality is intended to capture the way that modern governments produce the sort of citizens that they require through 'techniques of rule' that could be witnessed in schools, workplaces, hospitals, welfare systems, courts, and so on. In the early 20th century the projects in question were usually eugenicist, and were designed to improve the quality and quantity of the 'race', by confining or eliminating the weak, and through imperial expansion. By stressing that these programmes provided docile, efficient workers and mothers of future workers, Marxists (or ex-Marxists) could tap into new research without abandoning the core of their argument.

The strength of the Marxist approach is to relate fascism to the social struggles of the early 20th century, and to understand fascism in social action rather than just in abstract ideas. It illuminates the relationship between fascism and capitalism, and shows that the revolutionary discourse of fascists could mean something more conservative in practice. Marxists reveal the diverse material motives that attracted social groups to fascism, whether peasant farmers in the Po Valley or artisans in the Rhineland.

Marxists are right that many capitalists were delighted with fascists' destruction of the left. Yet it is not saying much to claim that fascism serves the interests of capitalism, for capitalism is such a powerful force that it can prosper under any regime that does not actually destroy it. Furthermore, whilst it can hardly be denied that capitalism and the market condition all aspects of modern society—the family, consumption, sport, for instance—it is equally true that family, consumption, and sport may influence the way capitalists understand their interests. Indeed, capitalists often disagreed on what their interests were, so we must explain why some capitalists believed that fascism served them, but others didn't.

Neither does the power of capitalism mean that it is the 'ultimate' explanation of fascism. In trying to make it so, Marxists are forced to relegate much of fascism to secondary status. For instance, they must play down the radical aspects of fascism. For Marxists, socialism is the only genuine form of radicalism. Consequently, they discount as 'rhetorical' the fascist movement's radical opposition to the established administrative elite and mainstream politicians. They fail to see its effects, and cannot account for fascists' willingness to ignore the wishes of business where they conflicted with other party goals.

The necessity of proving that fascism serves capitalism also causes Marxists to regard fascist territorial expansion and racism as secondary features of fascism. Some Marxists see these impulses as a cunning ploy to ensure that fascism's petty bourgeois supporters blame ethnic minorities rather than capitalists for their problems, or merely as the technically most advanced of capitalism's crimes (an updated Highland Clearance). Even if we accept the plausible contention that fascists used racism to undermine workers' class loyalties, it still stretches the point to argue for instance that capitalist defence required killing the mentally ill in Germany or Italianizing family names in South Tyrol. Perhaps fascists pursued these goals for reasons unrelated to the (supposed) logic of capitalism.

Weberian approaches

The next theory to be considered is often known as 'Weberian', although its roots in the eclectic sociology of Max Weber (1864–1920) are far from straightforward, and Weberian and Marxist interpretations of fascism possess some common ground. Nevertheless, the term 'Weberian' will be used for convention's sake.

Whereas Marxists held capitalists responsible for fascism, Weberians blamed the pre-industrial, or feudal, ruling class—the large landowners of Eastern Germany or the Italian Po Valley, the Latifundists of southern Spain, or the Japanese military caste. They argued that because these countries had not experienced genuine bourgeois and liberal-democratic revolutions, the old conservative elites played an exaggerated role in society. These 'traditional elites' used education and conscription to spread their reactionary values, and they resorted to ever more desperate means to preserve their positions. From the late 19th century, they sponsored mass nationalist movements in an attempt to undermine liberal democracy and socialism. German and Italian elites led their countries into the Great War in the hope that patriotic fervour would permit them to crush their domestic enemies. When that failed, they turned to fascism in a last-ditch attempt to save themselves. Fascism was primarily an antimodern movement, resulting from the convergence of pre-industrial elites with the petty bourgeoisie and peasantry. The latter groups were equally vulnerable to 'modernization', and so were open to the old elite's traditionalist propaganda.

Weberians also argue that the mass of the population becomes vulnerable to fascism when social change is particularly rapid, when traditional ways are eroded by 'modernization' or by war or economic crisis. As the old ways of doing things are undermined, people who placed their faith in tradition become disoriented (technically speaking, they suffer from 'anomie'). They turn to fascists, who promise to restore lost certainties. To the victims of modernization, fascism provides a total explanation of their place in the world; it explains the causes of change; identifies those responsible (foreigners and Jews, for instance), and provides a blueprint for restoration of a pre-modern utopia, which is totalitarian in character. Loosely speaking, these ideas underlie Ernst Nolte's contention that fascism is 'resistance to transcendence' (see earlier).

The strength of the Weberian approach is to have shown that the landed aristocracy, as much as capitalists, were immediately responsible for Mussolini and Hitler's accession to government. It is not wholly convincing, though, to regard fascism as 'antimodern', for it contained many features that others would see as modern. Some scholars defend the Weberian approach by saying that fascism pursued traditional ends using modern means. Too easily, scholars become mired in debates about what is 'modern', which are as futile as those about who is truly fascist.

Another difficulty is that the Weberian approach shares the Marxist assumption that the elites are able to manipulate the rest of the population—especially the petty bourgeoisie—at will. Like Marxism, Weberianism doesn't really account for the radical features of fascism. It pays more attention to fascist ideology than Marxism does, but reduces ideas to expressions of an undifferentiated desire for wholeness or utopia. As such, it shares weaknesses with our next theory of fascism.

Totalitarianism, political religions, and governmentality

The word 'totalitarianism' was invented by Italian Fascists to encapsulate their drive to 'nationalize' the Italian masses—to

11

incorporate them within a hierarchical, mobilized, militarized community serving the needs of Italy. As a scholarly concept, the term enjoyed its heyday in the 1950s and 1960s, when non-Marxist social scientists used the concept to link communism with fascism and thus discredit it.

Famously, the American political scientist C. J. Friedrich defined totalitarianism as follows:

1. A single mass party, led by one man, which forms the hardcore of the regime and which is typically superior to or intertwined with the governmental bureaucracy.

2. A system of terror by the police and secret police which is directed against real and imagined enemies of the regime.

3. A monopolistic control of the mass media.

4. Central control of the economy.

5. A near monopoly of weapons.

6. An elaborate ideology which covers all aspects of man's existence and which contains a powerful chiliastic [messianic or religious] moment.

Initially, researchers focused on points 1–4, that is on the structures of rule and the relationship between party and state. Point 5 we may pass over, since it makes sense only if one regards gun control as totalitarian. Point 6 is more important, for totalitarian theorists argued that fascism involved the revolutionary reconstruction of society in accordance with a utopian ideology, at a time when rapid change and crisis had encouraged people to seek a new way of making sense of the world. Utopianism always leads to terror. Since real people are far from perfectible they must be forced to assume their places in Utopia.

In the 1970s, the concept of totalitarianism fell out of use. The Cold War had thawed, and research demonstrated that far from representing a 'top-down' system of totalitarian control, Nazi and Fascist (and Communist) regimes were chaotic. However, in 1989, the collapse of communism revitalized totalitarian theory, for it once more became useful to identify the horrors of Stalinism with fascism. Meanwhile, the rise of postmodernism in Western universities revived scholars' interest in totalitarian ideology, for some postmodernists regard any all-encompassing system of ideas—whether based on religion, class, nation, or race—as intrinsically oppressive, a view that converges neatly with totalitarian theory's view that fascism attempts to create an ideal world according to absolute principles. Scholars of fascism rarely endorsed postmodernism, but they did participate in the turn towards the study of ideas, away from Marxist and Weberian concern with social structures.

Totalitarianism theorists answer critics of earlier versions by arguing that totalitarianism is an aspiration, which in practice did not achieve its ideals. The reality of chaos in fascist regimes is therefore quite compatible with totalitarian *intention*. Nevertheless, one finds the familiar assumption that rapid change dissolves the traditional world and creates the desire for a new integrating ideology, which fascists provide. In a striking metaphor, Michael Burleigh suggests that the Nazis sought to rebuild German society as engineers rebuild a bridge. They could not demolish it, since that would disrupt traffic, and therefore they replaced each individual part, so that passengers wouldn't notice.

Updated totalitarianism theory has three major strands. Roger Griffin sees fascism is a form of 'populist ultranationalism' which aims to reconstruct the nation following a period of perceived crisis and decline—he uses the Victorian term 'palingenetic', meaning 'rebirth from the ashes', to characterize fascism. This attempted national resurrection amounts to a revolution, in that fascism compensates for the destruction of tradition through the promotion of a modernizing, utopian ideology.

The second, complementary, version of totalitarianism is political religions theory. For Emilio Gentile, fascism's integrating ideology amounted to a secular religion. He argued that modernization caused the destruction of traditional religion, without undermining the mass's desire to believe. Fascism meets their need through sacralization of the party, state, and leader. This political religion, with its rituals, canonical texts, and high priests, also aims to create a 'new fascist man', who lives only for fascism, not for their family or for capitalism. Fascism is therefore revolutionary.

Totalitarianist approaches have also been combined with another strand of the diverse postmodernist movement: the previously mentioned concept of 'governmentality'. The techniques of rule developed by modern governments were allegedly so pervasive that they reached into all aspects of family, social, and bodily behaviour. And paradoxically, since people wanted economic success, education, and health, they coveted the very things that oppressed them, and thus colluded in their own oppression. Fascism could easily be seen as an intensification of governmentality, made possible by the destruction of enemies.

The advantage of these theories is to take seriously fascist ideas and plans. No longer can we say, as scholars once did, that fascism has no ideology (even if this ideology was more contradictory than totalitarian theorists allow). We may also agree that fascism could involve a revolutionary project of sorts; that it had something in common with religious fundamentalism; and that it pursued its goals with a violence justified by the conviction that opponents were part of a demonic conspiracy. Foucault's ideas have helped to stimulate a great deal of research on the role of doctors and other professionals and academics in fascism.

A major problem with the above theories is that they presume an undifferentiated and ultimately passive mass, integrated into fascism by ritual repetition of ideas and/or by technologies of rule.

Totalitarian theory is weak on why people join fascist movements. It confines itself to generalizations about anomie and the masses' desire for belief, and so cannot explain why particular groups were more likely to join than others were. In any case, no law dictates that an upheaval such as the Great War *must* lead to disorientation and isolation. On the contrary, the War also provoked a great upsurge of involvement in patriotic associations, out of which groups like the Fascists emerged. Responses to crisis were diverse, and they varied according to people's educational formation, social and religious position, age, and gender. One must seek the origins of fascism in the specific circumstances of specific groups. Insofar as the people who did espouse messianic ideologies came to power, we must ask why, and what they meant if and when they claimed that fascism was a religion.

Another problem is that totalitarian theory overstates the revolutionary side of fascism. In fact, it mirrors Marxists' exaggeration of fascists' conservatism. Totalitarianism theory holds that a totalitarian regime aims to destroy *all* alternative solidarities in the drive to create a new society. Such a dream is actually impossible to conceive, let alone implement, for it requires an impossible objectivity. Fascist leaders were divided on fundamental questions. Furthermore, prejudices and unacknowledged assumptions shaped their visions of Utopia and of what stood in the way of its achievement. Consequently, big business and the family (within limits) were more or less compatible with their understanding of the mobilized nation. Communism and feminism were not.

Totalitarianism is a useful concept only if we remember that it entails the urge to impose a worldview that is shaped by received ideas, and if we remember that fascists interpreted the totalitarian project in different ways. So we should not expect the fascist Utopia to differ completely from society as it presently exists. Indeed, there lay the appeal of fascism for many.

Burleigh's bridge metaphor is useful in that it suggests that ordinary people believed that fascism would repair the nation whilst leaving them to get on with their lives. It is inadequate insofar as fascists endeavoured to reconstruct the bridge according to a substantially modified blueprint, and the engineers quarrelled not just about what sort of bridge it should be, but about where it should begin and end. Their project demanded the mobilization of enormous resources, shook the bridge to its foundations, and threatened to derail the rolling stock. Yet many passengers happily lent a hand and acclaimed the engineers. Passengers and engineers agreed, moreover, that other passengers were secretly plotting to blow up the bridge, and as trains passed over the increasingly shaky bridge, thugs were throwing fare-paying passengers into the ravine below, under the half-averted gaze of fellow travellers, who wondered whether the murderers' uniforms were those of the usual guards.

Fascism as a synthesis of revolution and reaction

In the first edition of this book, I suggested a definition of fascism based on the fallacious assumption that by combining the advantages of Marxist, Weberian, and totalitarian theories one could arrive at a better definition of fascism. I gave due emphasis both to fascist ideas and to social context, and to revolutionary ambitions as well as reactionary agendas.

I argued that the contradictory nature of fascism stemmed from its origins. Most often, fascists were discontented conservatives. They were reactionary insofar as they were opposed to the left, socialism, feminism, and liberalism, which they saw as inimical to their material interests and values. They were revolutionary insofar as they thought that their own leaders had failed to defend conservative interests. The established ruling class should therefore be replaced by a new elite that would genuinely represent the national interest (as they saw it). Often, this rebellion revealed latent class and gender tensions among conservatives. More rarely, at least in the interwar years, fascism emerged from a crisis of the left. In that case, residual leftist hostility to the establishment jostled with the conviction that the left had betrayed the people—for example, by boarding the political gravy train. The mixed agendas of fascism explained why it took upon itself the task of destroying the left through paramilitary violence, but also threatened to displace the army. I also argued that fascism's contradictory origins explained its relations with other movements, for it possessed affinities with both left and right. Moreover, I argued that fascists combined violence against the left with re-working certain of its ideas and practices. For example, they suppressed left-wing trade unions, but established their own labour organizations; they opposed feminism, but set up women's groups in the party. Another advantage of the definition is that it allows for change; different elements of the fascist constituency set the tone in different circumstances.

Arguably, my definition better meets one of the tests of usefulness than the others: it explains more of what we know. It has all the advantages of the others, but it also explains further features, such as conflict within the movement and ambivalent relations with other movements. Yet my definition still glossed over some major differences between the cases that I claimed to explain. To support my contention that Fascism and Nazism belonged to the same category, I had to regard as secondary the exterminationist antisemitism of the Nazis. While there were similarities between Fascism and Nazism, it does not follow that Nazism was a form of fascism. In fact, my definition was as reductionist as any other, in that I sought to reduce the great richness and variety of actual movements and regimes to the priorities of my definition. In fact, I encountered problems that are intrinsic to all definitions. If we are to make progress we shall have to confront them.

The problem with definitions

To start with, any definition is selective: it privileges some aspects of fascism and leaves out others. Marxist and Weberian approaches emphasize conservative defence of material interests, while totalitarianism theory focuses on revolutionary ideas. Both sides assert (I stress 'assert') that their chosen criteria is more 'fundamental', but there is no way of deciding between these rival claims. Moreover, the diversity of fascism is such that any definition soon encounters evidence that does not fit. For instance, Marxists discover that some fascists attacked capitalism, while totalitarian theorists find that some fascists defended capitalism. Both use the same device to defend their theories. For Marxists, fascist anticapitalism was 'tactical', and was discarded in power; for totalitarianists, fascists' alliances with conservatives were 'tactical', and were discarded in power. My definition avoids those particular problems, but to defend it I had to reduce various aspects of Fascism and Nazism to derivations of the rebellion against established parties.

The necessity of selection also means that we have to choose whether to focus on leaders, party intellectuals, programmes, party members, voters, or perhaps all of them. Our definition will differ accordingly. Then we face the problem that people differed in their degrees of commitment to the movement. Some were just voters; some only read the party newspaper; some attended the odd meeting; some were fanatics. Many fascists also belonged to or sympathized with other parties. Moreover, people never defined themselves just by their allegiance to fascism. Those who belonged to fascist movements were never just fascists. They were also mothers, fathers, Catholics, atheists, workers, capitalists, and much more. However sophisticated our definition, it can never explain the history of an individual movement. For real people never acted simply as fascists, let alone according to our definitions.

Another problem is which 'cases' of fascism to include in our definition. Some scholars argue that we should derive our definition only from the original case, Italian Fascism. That choice has the apparent advantage of simplicity, but even then, one must decide which aspects of this heterogeneous movement and regime were definitional. Others urge us to base the definition on the two 'paradigmatic' cases—Fascism and Nazism. But why is Nazism paradigmatic and not, say, the Romanian Iron Guard or the Spanish Phalange? Once more, prior selection determines the definition. And the more cases we choose to include, the less they will have in common, the more general our definition will be, and the more awkward facts will have to be dismissed as 'secondary'.

With that in mind, some would say that Nazism is not really a form of fascism at all; it is better grouped with Communism, for both were 'totalitarian'. But choosing that categorization involves an equally arbitrary decision to privilege the methods of rule that Nazism and Communism shared, and to forget that Communism and Nazism had very different attitudes to private property, for instance.

Quite rightly, readers might ask what is the point of this book if it can't provide a once-and-for-all definition that enables them to recognize and understand fascism. If readers bear with me, I hope to show that our inability to pin fascism down does not mean that we can't say anything at all, or that it's all just a matter of opinion. Scepticism towards definitions does not mean that we can do without them altogether. To begin with, readers rightly expect me to tell them what I shall include in the book, but they must remember that what I include is a *choice*, and that I could have chosen differently. Thus, I cover movements and regimes that called themselves fascist or were called fascist by their enemies or by scholars. I made that choice because I suspect that readers will be interested in the ways in which these movements and regimes did or did not resemble fascism. What I do *not* claim is that one or more common denominators unite these movements, that they have a common core or dynamic. Otherwise put, *I use fascism as a convenient label, in the knowledge that it covers many meanings.*

19

The fact that our subject is a selection dependent on our interests need not be a problem, so long as we are as clear as possible what our definition can and cannot do (scholars rarely specify the latter). Each definition of fascism that I've discussed tells us *something*. Moreover, each of them is more compatible with the others than their advocates assume, but none can tell us *everything*—even if we combine them all. We cannot know what questions we will ask of fascism in the future (for instance, at one time nobody thought of researching the role of women in fascism, or fascism and the environment). Anyway, fascism is simply too diverse to pin it down.

That said, fascism is no more heterogeneous than any other political movement. But it is more than usually bogged down in questions of definition. We readily accept that 'socialism' or 'liberalism' can mean many different things in different circumstances, that they can overlap with other ideologies, and that activists can differ fundamentally on what their ideology means. We also recognize that debates over who qualifies as a 'true socialist' or as a 'true liberal' is part of the stuff of politics. How often is a party divided about who represents its 'real values' and who has 'betrayed' them? The crucial point is that the final meaning of a political label is ungraspable; more accessible is how a label is used in particular circumstances and what it means to protagonists. For instance, we may ask what Mussolini meant when he spoke of Fascism, how and why his views changed, and how they differed from those of other Fascists.

The only thing that really distinguishes fascism from other concepts is its enormous negative moral charge. Of course, other labels are used as insults—in the USA, 'liberal' can be pejorative. However, it is not hard to find people who regard any given label positively. In the case of fascism, few will assume the label, but the very gravity of the charge makes it a temptingly effective accusation to stick on opponents. Politicians and journalists use definitions as weapons, and fascism is a very good one. Furthermore, a definition is more effective as a slur if one can claim that it is 'objective' or 'scientific'. That's why protagonists often appeal to academics to arbitrate. Well-qualified scholars have been more than willing to respond, for many of them agree that one of their primary tasks is to establish exact definitions. In my view, academics are no better qualified to decide what 'true fascism' is than anyone else—as their inability to agree a definition amply confirms. Once they engage in the impossible task of defining fascism, they are sucked into the same undecidable definitional disputes that exercise politicians and journalists (often without resisting, it's true).

Academics *are* better equipped to explore the systems of political labelling that pertain in particular circumstances, how labels were used, and what they meant to protagonists. In that sense, the concept of fascism is essential to understanding the past: while *we* may be aware of the impossibility of defining fascism, *protagonists* believed that the concept was very real, and what they thought fascism was shaped their views and the way groups responded to each other. So rather than engage in the fruitless debate about whether Nazism was a form of fascism, we may explore the ways in which Nazis used the label or rejected it, how they interpreted the Italian regime, what they took from it, and how they combined their borrowings from Fascism with other ideas and practice.

Focusing on contemporary uses of the term 'fascism' does not mean that we can't also use our own concepts to understand fascism, so long as we're clear what we're doing. People are understandably interested in the question of how much present-day movements resemble fascism in the past, and I shall discuss that question. But we must remember that we are applying our own categories, and that we can only highlight similarities and differences—we can't say whether or not present-day movements *are* fascist in some deeper sense. We must also remember that we can't learn everything that there is to know about the movement that we are studying by categorizing it. Other definitions will show us different things.

Chapter 2
Fascism before fascism?

Aigues-Mortes, France, 1893

In the late 19th century, the saltworks of Mediterranean France were largely unmechanized, and the task of lifting salt was an exceptionally exhausting form of labour. Under the blazing August sun, workers pushed heavy barrowloads of salt along wooden planks to the top of ever-higher heaps of salt. Since the work was seasonal, poor itinerant workers performed it, and because France suffered from a shortage of labour, many of them were immigrant Italians.

On 16 August 1893, at the saltworks of Aigues-Mortes, unfounded rumours that Italians had killed three French workers triggered a veritable manhunt against the unlucky migrants. The next morning, the police escorted as many Italians as possible to the railway station. On their way, Frenchmen savagely assaulted frightened workers, killing at least six en route, and two elsewhere. Eventually, the Italians found refuge in the medieval Tour de Constance at Aigues-Mortes. No one knows how many more met anonymous deaths in the saltmarshes in the following two days.

Brawls between French and immigrant workers were common during this period, though not usually mortal. Antipathy to foreign workers marked all political tendencies—at Aigues-Mortes one column of French workers was headed by a red flag. Yet there was something novel about the Aigues-Mortes massacre.

By coincidence, Maurice Barrès, a writer seen by some as one of the inventors of fascism, had set his 1890 novel, *Le Jardin de Bérénice*, in Aigues-Mortes, and had used the Tour de Constance as the symbol of a new kind of nationalism. Barrès rejected the liberal and democratic view that the nation was the expression of the rational democratic choices of the individual (male) inhabitants of France to live together. For him, the nation emanated from a spiritual feeling beyond normal human reason—a view shaped by then trendy psychological ideas about the collective human unconscious, and by the literary symbolist movement, which believed that art could access the hidden myths underlying human behaviour (see Figure 1). Barrès saw the nation as the product of history, tradition, and the long contact of the peasantry with the national soil. From the top of the Tour de Constance, the hero of the novel sees the vastness of the French countryside. He communes with France's medieval past, and realizes that he, as an individual, 'is just a single minute in this vast country'. Barrès's hero was at one with the French soil. An immigrant never could be.

Barrès might seem to be just another self-obsessed artist, searching for the keys to the soul, and there is plenty of that in Barrès's writings. Yet there was more to him than this. In 1889, he had been elected to represent the eastern city of Nancy in parliament as a follower of General Boulanger, a soldier who had promised to cleanse France of corrupt parliamentary politicians. Barrès's electoral campaign, moreover, had exploited the antisemitism of the Nancy population. Increasingly, he saw nationalism as the solution to all problems. A few weeks before the Aigues-Mortes massacre, he wrote a series of pieces for the daily *Le Figaro*, under a headline that needs little elucidation: 'Against foreigners'. These articles were published at a time of poor relations between Italy and France, when Italian immigrants were

MAURICE BARRÈS

1. Maurice Barrès in 1888. Late 19th-century dress codes made it difficult for nationalist intellectuals to pose as men of the people. After the war, uniforms communicated the idea that activists were both part of the same community and situated in a hierarchy

regarded as potential spies. Barrès was not responsible for the events at Aigues-Mortes, but his novels and political journalism linked popular xenophobia with the intellectual origins of fascism. In 1898, Barrès referred to himself as a 'national socialist'.

These events raise the question of the origins of fascism, and even of whether fascism existed before fascism as we are discussing it here. Clearly, some pre-1922 movements were closer to fascism than others were. Yet we know little of the political preferences of those involved in the Aigues-Mortes massacre. And we can't draw a straight line from Barrès to fascism either, for his antisemitism and national socialism put him closer to Hitler than to Mussolini. Moreover, Barrès himself subsequently embraced conventional conservatism, and when war broke out, he celebrated the patriotism of Jewish soldiers.

Where to begin?

The discussion of definitions in the previous chapter complicates the search for the origins of fascism in the past. Remember first that defining 'fascism' involves selection among many different possibilities. If instead we classed Fascism and Nazism as totalitarian, we would have to hunt for antecedents of Communism too, and that would produce a very different story.

Second, starting with the foundation of the Fascists represents another choice. Indeed, it would make just as much sense to start with Nazism, and to ask whether Fascism was its precursor. Then again, we might take Barrès as the starting point, as the 'paradigmatic case'. That decision might have provoked us to depict Fascism and Nazism as variants of Barrèsian national socialism.

Third, the conflict over the significance and practical implications of key terms in the fascist lexicon and the diversity of motives that brought people to fascism suggest that its origins can't be found in a single place. Recognizing that puts paid to the view that Fascism and Nazism were outgrowths of something in the 'national traditions' or 'national psychology' of the Italians or Germans, or a response to the unusually great strains provoked by 'modernization' in either of those countries.

Rather than seek the origins of fascism in the past, we should look at the specific circumstances of Italy in 1919–22. During that period, the Fascists were casting around for ways to re-enter the struggle for power, to carve out a space, and compete with rivals. To that end, they used the ideas and traditions that they found around them—such as the idea of the fasces—and they created something new from them. Subsequently, foreign admirers would do the same: they would use fascism selectively along with other reference points to create an original, but contested, new synthesis. In this chapter, I shall examine some of the ideas on which both the Fascists and the Nazis drew. Unavoidably, I shall use hindsight to select relevant facts.

The same warning applies to another purpose of this chapter. I shall compare Fascism and Nazism to earlier movements and ideologies, highlighting those that anticipate various aspects of them. However, the existence of similarities does not mean that earlier movements 'caused' fascism, or that fascism existed latently, and just awaited favourable circumstances to become a mass movement or win power. We must not be fooled by apparent anticipations of fascism, for such is the eclectic and contradictory nature of any ideology that it is easy to find similarities between any two of them. If we compare past movements to fascism, then we will simply discover some similarities and some differences.

I shall emphasize that fascism drew on and transformed ideas from across the political spectrum. That's the only way to allow for the many disputes among fascists as to what fascism was. Furthermore, ideas, economies, societies, and political practices in Europe (and beyond) have always been so entangled that it is impossible to consider one country in isolation from another. All movements, in whatever country, whether of right or left, drew on ideas that hardly belonged to one country. Most 19th-century ideas contributed something to fascism, but none was intrinsically proto-fascist—not even those that most resembled fascism.

The conditions of fascism

That applies to the group of late 19th-century movements that scholars have designated 'the radical right'. They included the Pan-German League, the League of Patriots in France, the Italian Nationalist Association, and many others. Nobody used the radical-right label at the time, and the movements in question did not see themselves as belonging to a single category. On the contrary, they *believed* that nations were—or rather should be—unique, and they were dedicated to capturing power or influencing governments in their own countries. Yet the radical right drew on intellectual, political, social, and economic developments that crossed national frontiers and were, in some respects, shared with the left. They responded to similar pressures similarly, yet they re-worked common ideas and recombined them for their own purposes.

Let us begin with fascism's intellectual origins. If we reduce fascism to a political religion, we could trace it back to the radical sects of the Reformation or even the classical world, which prefigured the intolerant, illiberal, messianic mind-set of some fascists. But fascists arguably also owed something to quite different tendencies in religious history, such as the Scholastics' determination to use reason in the service of faith.

The Enlightenment of the 18th century is another potential starting point, but again the inheritance is complex. Fascism owed something to the Enlightenment idea that society need not be determined by tradition but could be organized according to a blueprint derived from universal principles. Historians influenced by Michel Foucault are sometimes keen to trace the fascist obsession with planning, medicalizing, and quantifying populations back to Enlightment science. The Enlightenment thinker Jean-Jacques Rousseau's notion that societies should be regulated by one such universal ideal, the 'general will', is also relevant. It was taken up by the most revolutionary of the French

Revolutionaries during the Terror of 1793, the Jacobins, some of whom justified violence as a means to construct an equal society and weed out those who opposed their plan. They were ready to force people to be free.

Yet fascism also owes a debt to those anti-Enlightenment thinkers who denied the validity of universal principles in the name of national traditions, as the German Gottfried von Herder did. French counterrevolutionaries, such as Joseph de Maistre, contended that 'natural' communities—nation, profession, and family—were more important than individual human rights were. Anti-Enlightenment philosophy had a great influence on 19th-century Romanticism, which repudiated reason in favour of nature worship, and counterpoised the genius of the artist to mass mediocrity.

Narrowing the focus, some situate the emergence of the radical right in the context of the 'revolt against reason', which was said to characterize the last decades of the 19th century. Certainly, many *fin-de-siècle* thinkers opposed rationalism and its ramifications: liberalism, socialism, materialism, and individualism. They were pessimists who refused to see history as progress, and instead saw it as a desperate struggle against degeneration. The fascist call for an elite to save the nation from degeneration—the idea of rebirth from the ashes (palingenesis)—emanated from this climate. In Germany, various strands of spiritualist thought, descended from Romanticism, informed the idea of the German '*volk*'—that is the people defined as an ethical, socially united, patriarchal, ethnic, and linguistic community. Barrès attacked rationalist republicanism in the name of a cult of ancestors and the soil.

Amongst those who influenced fascists, one must also cite the French theorist of crowd psychology, Gustave Le Bon, who held that irrational crowds could be manipulated by demagogues. Both Mussolini and Hitler cited Le Bon, but the man himself had been closer to conservatism, and his theories were as attractive to the left as they were to the extreme right. In Le Bon's mould was Georges Sorel, also cited by Mussolini, who argued likewise that the masses were motivated by myths and violence. Similarly, the Italian political scientists Gaetana Mosca and Vilfredo Pareto emphasized the role of force in preserving the political elite. The German philosopher Friedrich Nietzsche was convinced that universalism had undermined respect for the strong. He hoped that a man of destiny would create a more spiritual community, but his ideas were contradictory and eclectic. Scholars have disagreed about the extent to which any of these key thinkers were proto-fascist. The nub is that their ideas were appropriated and misappropriated by proto-fascists.

In fact we cannot see the origins of fascism exclusively in rejection of reason. On the contrary, the aforementioned thinkers all thought that myths, elites, and crowds could be studied using universal scientific principles. Le Bon, for instance, misused evolutionary science to argue that evolution and natural selection had permitted the elite to rise above the mass through development of the faculty of reason. Consequently, the elite could use social science to understand the origins of the mass's passions, and guide them in a safe, nationalist direction. By the standards of the time, eugenicist social planning, with its racist dimensions, was undoubtedly scientific. Of course, to us, much of this was pseudo-science.

Charles Darwin's principle of the survival of the fittest was, and remains, scientifically respectable, but its application to society was dubious. Social Darwinists feared that the comforts of modern society, coupled to assistance to the poor, would lead to survival of the unfit and social degeneration. They preached 'eugenicism' as the answer, proposing 'negative' measures such as sterilization of the unfit, and/or 'positive' reforms such as encouragement of reproduction of the healthy. Some Social Darwinists felt that only strong leaders could prevent the masses from succumbing to a late 19th-century equivalent of couch-potato syndrome. Social

Darwinists also believed that there was an inevitable struggle for power between nation-states, and sometimes felt that the fate of individuals was of little import compared to that of the nation.

Social Darwinism was allied to the even more questionable 'science' of race. The French monarchist Count Gobineau's 'Essay on the Inequality of Human Races', ignored since publication in 1853, began to be read in the 1890s. One admirer was the composer Richard Wagner, who blended antisemitism, Germanic Christianity purged of its 'Jewish elements', and paganism into an idealized Germanic myth. His son-in-law, Houston Stewart Chamberlain, added Social Darwinist and racist ideas. Hitler was a devotee of Chamberlain, and spent his life dreaming Wagnerian dreams of victory or death. Hitler denied, nonetheless, that Nazism was a religion—some of his speeches read like parodies of the dogmatic turgidity of 'scientific socialists' (i.e. Marxists).

Racism was an essential ingredient of imperialism. The carve-up in the 1880s and 1890s of Africa and much of Asia by the great powers stimulated national rivalries and promoted racism. Italian, German, and French nationalists believed that they had not won their fair share of empire, while defence of overextended empires was important to British ultranationalists. European powers used race science to justify domination over 'inferior' non-European peoples, and that permitted them to disregard the rule of law where they thought it appropriate. Extermination of some native peoples provided precedents for the Holocaust.

It is appealing, but facile, to draw direct lines between this climate and fascism. But fascism was only one of many possible consequences, and Mussolini's racism differed significantly from Hitler's. Moreover, many of the above ideas were used, in different ways, by moderate conservatives and the left. The British conservative Francis Galton and his left-wing pupil Karl Pearson, for instance, invented eugenics. The radical right was one emanation of a wide range of ideas, including mysticism and scientism, traditionalism and modernism, reason and unreason, which crossed political and national boundaries.

If we really want to explain how ideas such as these became embodied in the radical right, we must attend to context. To start with, this period saw the emergence of modern disciplines in the universities: history, sociology, political science, physics, biology, literary criticism, and so on. The rise of professional, specialized research led to displacement of old-style scholars, sometimes amateurs, who claimed scientific expertise in several fields. Lawyers and doctors, who had previously dominated university faculties, were especially likely to pretend to wide competence, and were attracted to the racist, eugenicist, psychological, and historical ideas described above. Doctors and lawyers were prominent in the far right. They claimed that their scientific training enabled them to pronounce on political and social questions.

Polymaths often resented their lack of recognition from specialist professional academics, and compensated by seeking political success. Some favoured the extreme left (the legally trained Lenin was a quintessential generalist) or moderate parties of left and right. Others preferred the new right. Barrès gave the republican establishment's refusal to honour a now-forgotten race theorist as a reason for entering politics. Jealousy of specialists was coupled with fear that professions were overcrowded with Jews and women. Doctors and lawyers espoused eugenicist theories, which they thought gave them the right to play god. Specialist academics were not immune from pseudo-scientific thinking and nationalism either. The point is that those who did believe that society could be modelled using scientific principles were attracted to political action, and they sometimes turned to the far right.

In particular, social and political scientists used crowd psychology and race to understand the advance of democracy—the much feared 'age of the masses'. All over Europe, from progressive

France to autocratic Russia, entitlement to the vote had been extended before 1914 (rarely to women). Public interest in elections grew, while mass, nationalist, socialist, Catholic, and peasant parties emerged. Alongside them sprouted multitudinous single-issue groups, from vegetarian societies to trade unions, women's groups, and colonialist lobbies. Technological innovations, such as the typewriter, railways, and telegraph, facilitated the growth of permanent national political organizations. For social scientists, the 'rise of the masses' was a problem to be solved, along with the question of how to preserve elite rule.

The radical right was both a consequence of mass politics and an attempt to contain it. It endeavoured to compete in that arena with its enemies, by placing nation above class or religion, repressing rivals, and taking over and re-shaping some left-wing policies. It is in the light of these potentially contradictory objectives that we should understand it.

The political origins of the radical right

Let's begin with nationalism. Hitherto, nationalists had largely been left-wing, for they advocated the rights of peoples to 'self-determination' and challenged the multinational Russian, Habsburg, and British states in the name of democracy. Often, though, nationalists combined this appeal to universal principles of justice with a potentially undemocratic romantic nationalism, which required quasi-mystical affirmation of the national idea by all inhabitants, who were supposed also to issue from the same racial origin and to be fundamentally different to other races.

The radical right was strong in countries where nationalists had recently established new states—Germany and Italy especially. Governments in these countries set about turning mere subjects into national citizens through education, linguistic conformity, conscription, and limitation of the influence of supranational churches. But radicals felt that governments had not done enough. The radical right was also strong in France, an old state, where a new Republic had been established in 1870. It too was keen to turn its peasant population into Frenchmen and to eliminate the influence of the Catholic Church, and it too faced challenges from more radical nationalists. In all these states, efforts to create a national community exacerbated competition for jobs and other rewards—as in the saltworks of Aigues-Mortes. Radical-right movements also emerged where ruling nationalities were threatened by separatist movements. In the Austrian part of the Austro-Hungarian Empire, the dominant Germans felt that too much had been conceded to Czechs and Poles. In Russia after the Revolution of 1905, the radical nationalist movement, the Black Hundreds, fought both national separatists and socialists.

Relations between the radical right and socialism were complex. On the one hand, a host of antisocialist organizations sprang up, including anti-Marxist trade unions, artisan associations, peasant leagues, and business groups, often linked to nationalist movements. On the other hand, there were potential meeting points between socialism and nationalism. For much of the century socialists had been nationalists, seeing themselves as representatives of the people and the nation, opposed to 'cosmopolitan' capitalists and aristocrats. Socialists blended into a wider radical tradition, which had rarely favoured rights for women and had sometimes been xenophobic. This exclusionary sub-current became more pronounced in the late 19th century in opposition to Marxism, for Marxists stressed internationalism rather than nationalism and factory workers rather than the people in general. Simultaneously, the emergence of feminism brought out implicit misogyny. Consequently, some socialists shifted from left to right.

Even orthodox socialists were not immune from the appeal of the radical right. Marxist orthodoxy taught that the bourgeois-democratic revolution must precede the victory of the proletariat. In Italy, which was still not democratic, some socialists thought that nationalism might bring about this essential precondition (that had been one of Mussolini's reasons for backing intervention in the War). Elsewhere, some socialists felt that their parties had become too bureaucratic and looked for alternative means to provoke revolution. Ex-socialist activists were not numerous in the radical right, and in Germany, they were nearly completely absent. However, we shall see that radical right and later fascism would attempt to re-work socialist ideas in order to reconcile the workers to the nation.

The radical right should also be considered in relation to the rise of feminism. Feminism was strongest in America, Scandinavia, and Britain, but was present to a greater or lesser degree in most European countries. In the 1890s, feminists became increasingly vociferous in their demands for access to the professions, and in the following decade turned their attention to the vote. The radical right was in the forefront of the male backlash. Yet the radical right also drew on religious organizations, in which women had traditionally played an important role. In addition, the radical right's recruits from socialism included some women. Again, the radical right would attempt to neutralize a threat by combining repression with re-working its opponents' ideas.

Conservatives were also attracted to the radical right—British conservatives connived with Carson's Ulster Volunteers, who opposed Home Rule for Ireland; Prussian Junkers founded the German Land League; French royalists funded the Antisemitic League during the Dreyfus Affair. Neither were liberals entirely opposed to the radical right, for many of them saw the egalitarianism of mass society as threatening hierarchy based on talent. They often regarded the market as akin to the Darwinian struggle for life, and they quietly accepted the ruin of lives in pursuit of the good of 'the economy'. Pareto, the Italian liberal academic whose lectures Mussolini might have attended, believed that the elite should not let humanitarianism obstruct the fight against socialism, and saw nationalism as a way to mobilize the mass for the collective good.

Conservative and liberal elites shared the radical right's hostility to feminism, socialism, and national minorities. Yet they were also ready to make concessions to their enemies, for they believed the 'rise of the masses' was an inevitable process with which they must compromise or risk political death. They participated in the radical right despite its radical tendencies, in the hope that they could divert demands for greater democracy into the lesser evil of a national mass movement.

Some radical right activists had different ideas. They did not believe that the established elites could defend the national interest, and it was true that governments, fearful of stirring up hysteria, often soft-pedalled national issues. The radical right called for governments more responsive to the needs of the people. In Germany, they condemned 'courtly Byzantinism', and demanded 'the elevation of all parts of the nation to consultation and participation in national matters'—paradoxically through a strong leader. In the German, French, and Italian countryside, pastors and priests (once regarded as bulwarks of the established order) stirred up the peasantry. In its own way, the radical right 'democratized' conservative politics.

The radical right did not, then, derive simply from ultranationalism or anomie. It was rooted in daily contests for jobs, financial reward, educational success, and political honour against socialists, ethnic minorities, feminists, and liberals, in a context of nation-building and imperialism, and interest in improving the quality and efficiency of the race. In these struggles, radical nationalists re-worked the ideas that they found to hand, taking them from all parts of the political spectrum. That does not mean that the radical right was 'neither left nor right', for in the specific context of the period, they found allies and political opportunities on the right more than the left, as the examples discussed below demonstrate.

These examples represent only a selection of the many radical-right movements that could be found before 1914. It is difficult to say which, if any, was the first radical-right movement. None resemble fascism completely, and that there were many dead ends. Few scholars have detected the origins of fascism in Italy or Germany, but some not entirely convincingly, have looked to France. Perhaps closest to certain strands of interwar fascism were the Ku Klux Klan, created just after the Civil War by Confederate Officers, who were alarmed the prospect of African-American equality. They were probably the first to wear a uniform; they engaged in violence against the race enemy, and they created something like a parallel authority. Even they lacked the corporatist and imperialist dimensions of fascism.

France

There is no denying that France provided a favourable terrain for the radical right. National sentiment had been wounded by defeat at German hands in 1870 and by getting the worst of imperial conflicts with Britain. Revolution was notoriously frequent in France, and now Marxist socialism and revolutionary trade unionism seemed to threaten the onset of another revolution. The word 'feminism' was first used in France in 1872. Republican governments endeavoured to construct a unitary, secular national state on liberal-democratic principles, but they faced resistance both from Catholics and from those who thought that national unity was incomplete. France's need for immigrants to work in its agriculture and industry stimulated popular xenophobia, as at Aigues-Mortes.

The French radical right resulted from the meeting of four tendencies of unequal importance:

- royalists and Catholics marginalized and radicalized by successive defeats at the hands of republicans;
- Catholic populists desperate to resist secularization and capture leadership of the proletariat from the socialists;

- nationalists annoyed by the government's apparent lack of interest in revenge against Germany;
- the nationalist and populist wing of socialism, of which Barrès attempted to capture the leadership.

Socially, the appeal of the radical right ranged from *déclassé* aristocrats like the antisemitic Marquis de Morès, through shopkeepers who resented 'Jewish' department stores in Paris, to xenophobic workers who joined 'Yellow' trade unions during the 1900s.

Italy

Italy was unified between 1859 and 1870 through military action by the state of Piedmont and its French ally, rather than by a popular nationalist movement. Some nationalists felt that Italy had not been truly unified. Italy was indeed governed by an oligarchy of (conservative) Liberals. The franchise was limited and Catholics refused to participate in elections because unification was achieved at the expense of Papal rule over central Italy. Furthermore, Italy had experienced military defeat in Abyssinia in 1896, parliamentary scandals, working-class unrest in the north, occupation of landed estates by poor peasants in the south, and in 1900, assassination of the king.

Convinced that repression of unrest was ineffective, the progressive Liberal, Giovanni Giolitti, prime minister from 1901, set about wooing moderate socialists and Catholics to his government. Nationalists were outraged by Giolitti's overtures to 'unpatriotic' socialists. In 1910, they came together in the Italian Nationalist Association (INA). This group received support from big business, the administration, and academics, but recruited largely from the middle classes, including lawyers and especially teachers, of whom the future philosopher of fascism Giovanni Gentile was one. Teachers had led the struggle to 'make' Italians.

The INA evoked the great 19th-century patriot Mazzini's nationalism, yet stripped it of its liberal humanism, and preached that national unity could be achieved only by an authoritarian state. Achieving unity entailed suppression of Socialist organizations and enrolement of workers into new corporatist bodies, loyal to the Italian nation. The INA also wanted to refashion the nation through war. The intellectual Enrico Corradini called for 'feminine' liberal internationalism to give way to 'male' virility. He didn't see war as a means to secure precise foreign-policy objectives, or to obtain markets and raw materials, but to integrate all classes into the nation through permanent expression of patriotism.

There were some affinities between the INA and revolutionary syndicalist trade unionists. Some syndicalist intellectuals had become convinced by the failure of strike movements that socialism was impossible in contemporary Italy. They held that a genuine national state must be created before the proletariat could take power, and they agreed with nationalists that war might help achieve this objective. In any case, syndicalists often believed in 'the people' more than the proletariat. Mussolini would eventually take over some of these ideas.

Germany

Germany, too, had been unified in 1866 to 1871 'from above', thanks to Prussian armies. It was governed by elitist conservative nationalists and right-wing liberals, who espoused anti-Catholicism, antisocialism, and antifeminism.

The belief that Germany had been incompletely united flourished. Julius Langbehn's anonymously published *Rembrandt as Educator* (1890) was a perfect example of *völkische* thinking—that is, of a nationalism rooted in an ethnically united people. Langbehn believed that the Dutch master, like his fellow countrymen, was actually German by race, and his chaotic book depicted Rembrandt as the teacher of a new German reformation.

Langbehn epitomized amateur generalists—he nourished a grievance against the 'dissipation' of science into specialization. He advocated combining science with art, and replacing dry professional history with a history informed by the psychic reality of race. He invoked both contemporary eugenic science (holding that if Berlin bars were replaced by public baths, socialism would be washed away) and the myth of the artist-hero, rooted in the *volk*, who would complete political unity with spiritual rebirth.

Langbehn's new Reformation required suppression of political divisions, revival of more 'virile' (and heretical) Germanic Christianity, and treatment of Jews as 'poison'. Langbehn's book sold enormously well. Even Catholics welcomed its critique of progressive ideas, despite Langbehn's blasphemy and identification of Germany with the Protestant peasantry. In the late 1920s, sales of Langbehn's work revived. Notably, he, along with others of the radical right more generally, had anticipated the Nazi's shift away from traditional imperial ambitions in Asia and Africa towards expansion in Eastern Europe, harnessed also to the idea of *lebensraum* (living space). Langbehn's project brought together schemes for racial, social, and eugenic engineering with the idea that Germany must develop a power bloc able to compete economically and militarily with American, British, and Russian rivals.

Many elite conservatives took seriously the radical-right programme. They shared the ultranationalists' enemies, joining the League of Struggle Against the Emancipation of Women and the Imperial League Against Social Democracy. They harnessed nationalist demagogy to the defence of material interest; they sponsored the populist, antisocialist, and antisemitic Agrarian League to win peasant support for protectionist tariffs, and the Eastern Marches Society to agitate for the conquest of new agricultural land in the east at the expense of Poles. More than the radical nationalists did, they prioritized empire outside Europe. Business interests, wealthy professionals, and government officials backed the Pan-German League and the Navy League in the belief that colonialism would consolidate the German state and expand markets.

Popular nationalism counted too. The Agrarian League had been built partly from peasant associations, such as those led by Otto Böckel, the 'King of the Peasants', which blamed Jews, cities, priests, doctors, the state, and the aristocracy for their problems. At its Tivoli conference in 1893, the German Conservative Party incorporated antisemitism into its platform in the hope of defusing this discontent. Likewise, when the conservative government launched its naval building campaign in 1896 it relied for propaganda upon the Pan-German League. Yet the Pan-Germans went further than the government liked in its attacks on Catholics and the British. By 1902, under the leadership of Heinrich Claβ, the Pan-Germans saw the foundations of the nation as much in the *volk* as in the monarchy. In 1913, Claβ argued that only a strong leader could save Germany, a programme summed up in his pamphlet 'If I were Kaiser'.

Russia

During the 1905 Revolution, Russian conservatives reacted against the upsurge of socialism and national separatism. The Union of the Russian People—better known as the Black Hundreds—was sponsored by the administration and Tsar, who shared its delusion that the revolution was the work of Jews. With the connivance of the authorities, the Black Hundreds contributed to hundreds of pogroms, in which over 3,000 Jews were murdered. Notwithstanding collaboration with the old right, the Black Hundreds were appalled by the Tsar's apparent inability to deal with the left, and wished to install a 'popular autocracy'.

Britain

The profoundly divided pre-1914 British Conservative Party included an outspoken minority of ultranationalists. The triumph of the Liberals in 1906, their reduction of the powers of the House of Lords and the introduction of the welfare state, along with the rise of Labour, strikes, and suffragette demonstrations, seemed to presage revolution. The passage of an Irish Home Rule Act seemed to foreshadow the break-up of the United Kingdom. Ulster's resistance to Irish Home Rule stimulated radical nationalism there, and many Conservatives sympathized with it. Some accused German-Jewish financiers of plundering the nation, while in London's East End a Brothers League with 45,000 members attacked Jews seeking refuge from pogroms in Russia.

From the radical right to Fascism?

This survey, although incomplete, shows that radical right movements and ideas were widespread. They provided models on which fascists would draw, but they weren't direct precursors. Fascists would not look exclusively to the radical right for inspiration. The radical right was perhaps stronger in France where fascism never triumphed than in Italy or Germany. In Germany, there was no clear geographical correlation between support for populist peasant groups in the 1890s and backing for the Nazis later.

There were significant differences between the radical right and fascism. Except perhaps in France, the radical right rarely wanted power in its own right. More often, it sought to stiffen existing regimes. Some activists fought their enemies in the streets, but no radical right group possessed the paramilitary formations of the interwar years. In France, the major far-right group in the 1900s, Action française, placed its faith in disciplined minorities, of whom it expected a coup that would restore the monarchy and establish orderly government, which it believed were embodied in the Catholic Church and classical aesthetics.

The Great War, the peace treaties, and the economic difficulties of the interwar years fundamentally changed the situation.

It opened up unprecedented opportunities for the revision of frontiers. For Germany, the collapse of Russia seemed briefly to make the acquisition of *lebensraum* possible, only for the alleged 'stab-in-the-back' on the part of the new socialist government to snatch away the opportunity. Meanwhile, the defeat of the Central powers encouraged the Romanians, Italians, French, and others to make claims on German and Austro-Hungarian territories that were not always satisfied, but outraged the defeated. Simultaneously, the Russian Revolution provoked immense fear in conservative Europe, especially as communist movements sprouted in Hungary, Finland, France, and Germany. Not only did communism promise the destruction of capitalism, but of the family, and it took up the cause of ethnic minorities all over Europe.

Again, there was no direct link from anticommunism to fascism. On the contrary, beleaguered governments made substantial concessions to nationalists, peasants, socialists, and women in a bid to win support for war efforts. As the War ended, popular discontent and uprisings all over Europe frightened governments even more, but their response was usually to reinforce democracy and make further concessions.

In Germany, Italy, and elsewhere, new mass movements opposed these many-headed threats and denounced conservatives for conceding too much to them. Often the new groups were paramilitary for they grew out of veterans groups, and they attracted people who had been brutalized by war and civil war. Not all old soldiers worshipped force—many became pacifists. Yet the appearance of movements such as the Fasci di Combattimento was clearly a product of the War.

Wartime government intervention had also reinforced the conviction of politicians, intellectuals, and journalists that science, state planning, and engineering of the population could restore national greatness, an idea grafted onto the Social Darwinist

42

conviction that the nation must struggle for life in a competitive international situation. Preservation of national strength often implied economic self-sufficiency behind tariff walls, repression of socialism and incorporation of the workers into the national community, encouragement of women to have babies for the nation, and assimilation or expulsion of ethnic minorities.

It is impossible to understand fascism without taking into account the upheaval of the Great War and the subsequent crisis. And given that experience of war and revolution crossed national boundaries, and was understood using a common fund of ideas, it is not surprising that movements resembling Italian Fascism emerged more or less independently of each other in several countries, without using the name. No national tradition was immune from these developments. So why did Fascism win power in Italy? After all, Italy was a victor country; Germany had been defeated. True, Italians claimed that their victory had been 'mutilated', but so, quite soon, did French nationalists. The postwar economic crisis in Italy was probably less serious than the Great Depression would become in Germany, Britain, or the USA. At the time of its advent to power, the Italian Fascist Party had fewer members than other groups that would never get close to power. Only analysis of specific circumstances can solve the problem. In all countries there were women and men who in one way or another anticipated aspects of fascism. Why did they become significant threats to democracy in some countries and not others?

Chapter 3
Italy: 'making history with the fist'

Rome, 16 November 1922

Although there were only 32 Fascists in the chamber, Mussolini was supremely confident that his new government would secure parliamentary approval. Journalists found him in expansive mood, posing as a man of will and decision. He obviously delighted in the luxury hotel in which he had taken up residence, with his shabbily dressed armed guard.

It was unclear what Fascism would mean in practice. The Blackshirts had not staged the 'March on Rome' to see Mussolini become another high-living prime minister in the Liberal state. They expected a thoroughgoing 'national revolution'. Yet Mussolini did not owe his elevation to the Blackshirted *squadristi* alone, for ruling liberal politicians had offered Mussolini the premiership well before the Blackshirts arrived in the capital. Who would have the upper hand—the Blackshirts or the conservatives?

Then there was Mussolini himself. He told a *Times* journalist that he intended to improve living standards for the poor, and that the bourgeoisie had some nasty surprises in store. Others learned that he would proclaim himself 'the prince of reactionaries' and create a special ministry of police, or that he intended to bend the people to his will in a new national community. Mussolini was hardly less contemptuous of his own lieutenants than he was of Liberal politicians.

Mussolini's speech in parliament clarified little. He multiplied assurances to the establishment, claiming that constitutional government was safe. Yet he threatened deputies with Fascist revolutionaries if they refused to grant him special legislative powers. Observers domestic and foreign felt that something unprecedented had happened in Italy, but they were uncertain what it was.

The rise to power

In 1915, the Interventionists had their way, and Italy entered the war, but the experience did not create the national unity they expected. The Socialist Party maintained its opposition to the war throughout—unlike its European counterparts. Levels of unionization grew and strikes were numerous. Over 600,000 men were killed, defeat succeeded defeat, and demoralization spread through the army. The war also seemed to invert normal relations between the sexes, for women had taken over some male jobs. Soldiers believed that women were more interested in profiting from the absence of menfolk than in aiding the war effort.

Defeat at Caporetto in October 1917 belatedly galvanized public opinion, permitting Italy to hold out for the rest of the war. In the peace treaty, much territory was won from Austria, though inevitably not as much as the nationalists wanted. Outraged, D'Annunzio, at the head of a band of veterans, seized the Adriatic port of Fiume in September 1919, and was not expelled until December 1920s (see Map 1).

Continued social unrest exacerbated nationalist anger. In 1918–20 (the 'Red Years'), strikes with factory occupations were common in

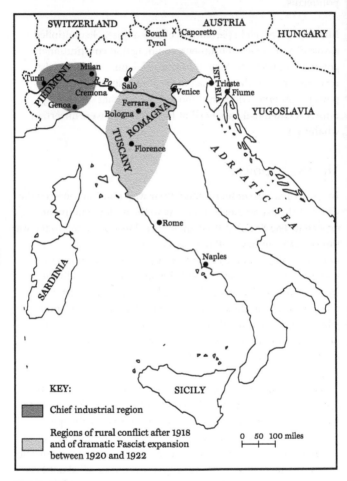

Map 1. Italy

the cities of the north, while in the Po Valley, agricultural labourers and peasants engaged in strikes, and in the south landless labourers occupied uncultivated land. In border regions Slav and German minorities demanded autonomy. The women's movement had been stimulated by involvement in the war effort, and the lower house of parliament approved women's suffrage, but the measure did not become law.

In the general elections of 1919, Socialist and Catholic Parties made major gains. Secular Liberals formed a series of administrations with Catholic support. These governments were paralysed by divisions between hardliners and compromisers behind Giolitti, Catholics and secularists, Interventionists and neutralists. The usual way of resolving crisis through formation of a new parliamentary coalition was impossible. Agitation in the factories and countryside and the divisions of the elite disrupted the old political routines, creating a more than usually fluid situation. The options became harder to read and the consequences of choices were harder to predict, but people did not become irrational. Rather, fascism succeeded because it bridged the gap between parliamentary manoeuvres and popular mobilization.

In 1921, Fascism took off in regions affected by agrarian unrest, where the youthful rural bourgeoisie began to join in large numbers. These sons of estate managers, small-town officials, and teachers, many of them veterans, saw in fascism a way to fight the Socialist and Catholic leagues, the government having failed to do so. They won the support of many conservative small peasants and landless labourers, who agreed that the authorities were not protecting them from the left. Fascist squads (*squadristi*) began a violent campaign of intimidation against Catholics and especially Socialists, in which many hundreds were killed. Meanwhile Fascists fought Slav minorities in the Venezia Giulia, and expanded in the cities, where they helped break a general strike in July. By 1922, the Fascists had effectively taken over the administration in many rural areas, and possessed a quarter of a million members.

Already there were tensions within the movement. Landowners and businessmen, who despaired of government support against strikers, provided encouragement and paid for the petrol that transported the squads. Other Fascists were dismissive of the 'feminine' softness of the bourgeoisie. They announced the advent of a manly elite, tempered by war, ready to do whatever was necessary to defeat the nation's enemies. Although others might have regarded them as bourgeois, the Fascists castigated the idleness of the bourgeoisie, and saw themselves as representatives of those who a worked—those who were 'competent' to govern the country and create a new Italy. Fascists were as likely to fight conservative nationalists on the streets as to collaborate with them. Mussolini remained reluctant to cut all ties with the Socialists. And whereas the wealthy were content just to see Socialist and Catholic organizations destroyed, Fascists set about forming unions of their own. They drew upon a pre-existing fund of conservatism amongst some peasants and workers, while carrot-and-stick methods encouraged more to join. Conservatives were reassured when in late 1921 Fascism became an organized party, the Partito Nazionale Fascista (PNF), and embraced monarchism and liberal economics.

In the summer of 1922, grassroots Fascist pressure for the capture of power intensified, and plans were laid for a 'March on Rome' (see Figure 2). Mussolini knew that a coup was risky, given the potential resistance of the army and what remained of the left. He owed his victory to the fact that he alone linked the mass movement to parliamentary politics. He carefully cultivated a national image by confining his journalistic output to Italy's place in the world, and benefitted from the discrediting of his rival, D'Annunzio, in the Fiume expedition. He was the only national figure who possessed authority in the mass movement.

2. The March on Rome: Mussolini and his lieutenants arrive in Rome, 28 October 1922. From left to right, Italo Balbo, Mussolini, Cesare Maria De Vecchi and Emilio De Bono

Liberal politicians faced a thorny choice. If they resisted, the army and police might refuse to fight the Fascists. Even if the Fascists were defeated, the left might profit. Politicians, business, and army agreed that it was better to bring the Fascists into the government, even though they possessed few seats in parliament. Fascist participation might harden the authorities' resolve against the left and revitalize the body politic. Mussolini became prime minister on 29 October 1922.

Fascism in power

Assured of the support of administration and army, Fascists attacked the left with impunity, and the extreme violence they used against their enemies must be remembered in any discussion of the subsequent 'consent' of Italians to the new regime. In 1923, the Catholic party, the *Popolari*, disintegrated under the dual impact of *squadristi* attacks and the removal of Papal support—Mussolini promised the Papacy improvement in the

Church's position in return for this favour. Beyond this, it was uncertain what Fascism stood for. Somewhat artificially, we may isolate three possibilities, but in fact, alliances shifted according to the prominence of issues.

Now that the Party was in government, conservatives flooded into it, reassured by repression of the left and espousal of liberal economics. They hoped that Mussolini would re-establish order, and that 'normalization' would follow. They wanted a more authoritarian version of the old system, in which their own social and political power would be guaranteed, but they believed parliamentary government and a degree of political liberty to be essential to the maintenance of their influence. In 1923, Fascism also absorbed the Italian Nationalist Association (INA), which wanted a more authoritarian state, and had long advocated incorporation of Catholics into the nation. They were not enamoured of disorderly *squadristi*, but had created similar groups of their own. Other Fascists called for a 'second revolution' to displace established politicians. The diverse radicals included syndicalist intellectuals and Fascist trade union leaders, feminists, local Party bosses hungry for power, and economic modernizers.

Dictatorship

Mussolini did not side clearly with any tendency. However, he did alter the electoral law so that Fascists won a parliamentary majority in 1924. During the campaign, the Fascists again used violence against the Socialists, but went too far when they murdered their spokesman, Giacomo Matteotti. Mussolini was implicated in the crime and there was an outcry even from hitherto supportive Liberals. Initially, Mussolini made concessions to his critics, but that only intensified calls for a 'second revolution'. Fascist unions piled on the pressure against business, while Fascist women renewed demands for the vote.

In January 1925, Mussolini bowed to radical pressure and declared his intention to install a genuinely Fascist regime. Fascism remained diverse, though, because Conservatives did not leave, for they feared recovery of the left if Mussolini fell. At the end of the year political opposition was banned, freedom of the press ceased, and election of local government ended.

Fascism became dictatorial, but factionalism continued. The heirs of the INA remained powerful, and they wanted a strong state to nationalize Italians and restore bourgeois society through discipline and hierarchy. Influenced by German philosophy, they held that individual freedom was meaningful only where a strong *state* expressed the national interest. The INA opposed demands for *party* supervision of the administration, army, and civil service. They insisted that Fascists obey the law rather than make it up.

The INA stalwarts Luigi Federzoni, as interior minister in 1926, and Alfredo Rocco, as justice minister from 1925 to 1932, helped lay the foundations of the regime. Fascist violence gradually ended. The state set up its own youth and women's organizations in an attempt to realize the INA's dream of the 'nation-mobilized-from-above'. Established interests, including the monarchy, big business, and agrarians retained much influence. In 1929, Mussolini delivered on his promise to the Pope. The Lateran Pact ended six decades of papal opposition to the Italian state, and accorded the Church considerable rights in education and youth work.

The brutal grassroots rural fascism epitomized by Roberto Farinacci, leader in Cremona, was weakened. By the late 1920s the prevailing image of the fascist was no longer the young, single man who fought Socialists while professing not to 'give a damn', but the responsible husband and father who worked from nine to six building a new nation, while his wife bore babies for Italy. During these years, those who saw Fascism as a vehicle for the realization of feminist demands, or for autonomous trade unionism within a corporatist economy, were frustrated (see Chapters 9 and 10).

However, Fascist radicals were never marginalized, even if radicalism acquired new meanings. The regime didn't become just another of the royal-bureaucratic dictatorships so common in interwar Europe (see Chapter 6). Mussolini never wanted such a regime, and so he used the Party as a lever against conservatives. The Party remained independent, and never abandoned its desire for control over welfare, education, and leisure—for the mobilized nation.

Farinacci, now general-secretary, played an ambiguous role. His backing for a centralized dictatorship inadvertently reduced the freedom of action of local Fascist radicals. Yet Farinacci simultaneously encouraged the Party to bypass bureaucratic methods of government and create a new ruling class. He was soon ousted, but his successors, Augusto Turati and Achille Starace, pursued the same goals more circumspectly. The unintended result was to turn the Party into an inflated parallel bureaucracy, and a party card became a prerequisite of advancement in state service. Often civil servants merely paid lip service to Fascist ideals, but the essential point is that access to power in the Fascist state depended as much on ideological conformity as on the normal methods of selecting and training bureaucrats. In 1932, Mussolini demanded that graduates of the Fascist Academy of Political Sciences (created in 1928) be given state jobs. Fascists wanted ideology rather than rules to become the basis of administration.

In effect, there was a stand-off. The Party, along with big business, the Church, state, army, Fascist unions, and corporations formed several semi-autonomous power centres in Fascist Italy. There was much rivalry and confusion between them. For instance, the Fascist workers' leisure organization, Dopolavoro, began as a state organization, but in 1927, the Party took it over in an attempt to undermine the influence of Fascist unions over workers. Dopolavoro still had to compete with Catholic organizations and Fascist trade unions for workers' loyalties, however. Similar conflicts marked the history of women's and youth organizations.

The Duce wanted the final say in all disputes, and so he pored over state papers in his study until the small hours. At one time, he nominally headed eight ministries. Obviously, he couldn't really decide everything. His interventions were haphazard, ill-prepared, and there was plenty of room for others to act. Mussolini was nevertheless essential to the regime. His power, when he chose to exercise it, was immense. He was considerably more popular than any of his lieutenants, none of whom could risk directly contradicting the Duce. Mussolini's power was especially strong in foreign affairs, the one area he chose unambiguously to make his own. In the 1930s, the drive to war inaugurated another, different, radicalization of the regime.

Mussolini's foreign adventurism was the fruit of three factors. First, Fascists had always seen the conquest of new territory as the best means to resolve economic problems, and regarded war as intrinsically good for the nation. Second, fascistization of the Foreign Ministry overcame its caution. Although Mussolini's foreign policy had precedents in the pre-Fascist epoch, it was marked by Fascist ideology. Expansion was justified by the Darwinian struggle between nations, and by the need for Italy to find living space for surplus population.

Third, Hitler's advent to power transformed the situation. At first, Mussolini saw Germany as a dangerous rival. He resented Nazi influence in foreign movements that had formerly admired Fascism. He was wary of German expansionism, not least because he feared that German-speaking minorities in South Tyrol might come into Hitler's sights should he annex Austria to the Reich. Yet some Fascists cited Nazism to justify demands for more radical polices, reversing the direction of influence between Italy and Germany. Moreover, Mussolini himself soon realized that the only way to expand Italian power was in alliance with Hitler, at the expense of British and French interests in the Mediterranean and Africa. Italian armies invaded Abyssinia in 1935, and found that only Germany backed them. The two regimes signed the Axis alliance in 1936, and on a visit to Berlin in the following year, Mussolini declared that 'Fascism and Nazism are two manifestations of the parallel historical situations that link the life of our nations'. Fascists and Nazis fought on General Franco's side in the Spanish Civil War (1936–9). In 1940, Italy joined the invasion of France, once it became clear that Germany would win, and, in 1941, invaded Greece and began an advance on Egypt.

Gearing up the nation for war coupled with the challenge of the Great Depression and alliance with Germany, shifted Fascist priorities and reshaped its factions. To achieve economic self-sufficiency, the regime increased regulation of the economy and intervention in private life. The population was encouraged to eat home-grown rice rather than imported pasta—a nation of spaghetti eaters, Mussolini declared, could never restore Roman civilization. Meanwhile, a state holding company, the Istituto per la Ricostruzione Industriale (IRI), established *de facto* control over failing firms; in 1936, the large banks were nationalized. These measures did not threaten big business per se. In fact, very large concerns gained at the expense of smaller competitors. Yet business became enmeshed in the sort of state controls that it had hoped to avoid by helping the Fascists into power.

War also reinforced efforts to mobilize the population. Under Starace, secretary from 1931 to 1939, the Party 'went to the masses', enrolling huge numbers of women and students. Starace organized ritual adoration of Mussolini in mass demonstrations, and took special interest in the regulation of workers' leisure in the Dopolavoro. The invasion of Abyssinia had already demonstrated the regime's capacity for racism. To counter

German influence in Romanian and Hungarian sister parties, Mussolini attempted to strengthen links with antisemites there. In 1938, antisemitic laws were introduced in Italy, as much in a spirit of competition as in emulation of Nazism. Many had doubts about antisemitism, but nonetheless the regime would later participate in the Holocaust.

The totalitarian intention behind these measures is clear, but little was actually achieved. Policies were implemented haphazardly, and in any case, Italy may not have had the infrastructure required for all-embracing regulation of social life. Worse, from the regime's point of view, 'going to the people' alarmed business, Church, and monarch. The strategy did not win the people either, for discontent grew as the war brought defeats, bombing, and food shortages. The gap between propaganda and practical achievements was obvious.

The Italian war effort was unimpressive. The people had no stomach for war. German assistance was required to rescue Mussolini's forces in Greece and North Africa. In 1943, the Allies invaded Italy, and the Fascist Grand Council and King conspired to evict Mussolini from office. Italy became a battlefield, with Germany occupying the north and the Allies the south. The Duce was imprisoned, but was soon rescued by German forces, who installed him as head of the Salò Republic in northern Italy. Die-hards attempted to implement Fascism in its allegedly 'pure' form, strongly influenced by Nazism, whilst engaged in armed struggle with the Resistance. Neither side showed any reluctance to fight.

Chapter 4

Germany: the racial state

Germany, 23 March 1933

The opening session of parliament, the Reichstag, took place in
the Kroll Opera House, on the Tiergarten in central Berlin, for the
Reichstag building had burned down a few weeks previously.
Inside the hall, a huge swastika flag hung behind the platform
occupied by the cabinet and president of the Reichstag. To get in,
deputies had to run the gauntlet of insolent swastika-wearing
youths massed on the wide square in front, who shouted 'Centrist
pigs' or 'Marxist sows' at them. Communist deputies had been
imprisoned because of the Party's alleged involvement in burning
down the Reichstag. A few Socialists were also incarcerated and
another was arrested on entering the building. Nazi stormtroopers
lined up behind the Socialists and blocked the exits.

Only one item lay before the Reichstag: an enabling law, giving
the Chancellor the power to legislate without Reichstag approval,
even where laws violated the constitution. Since the law entailed a
constitutional change, a two-thirds majority was required, and the
Nazis therefore needed conservative support. Hitler's speech
introducing the proposed law reassured conservatives that neither
the existence of parliament nor the position of their icon,
President Hindenburg, were threatened. It was understood that
conservatives would vote for the Enabling Act.

Frowning intensely, Hitler read his declaration with an unusual self-possession. Only in calling for public execution of the author of the Reichstag fire, and in uttering dark threats against the Socialists, did his notorious frenzy surface. At the end of his speech, Nazi deputies thundered out 'Deutschland über alles'.

In reply, the Socialist Otto Wels courageously recalled the 'principles of humanity and justice, of freedom and socialism'. The French ambassador remembered that Wels spoke with the air of a beaten child; his voice choking with emotion, he concluded by a thought for those already filling concentration camps and prisons. Hitler, who had been feverishly taking notes, passionately responded by accusing Socialists of having persecuted the Nazis for 14 years. In fact, Nazis had been punished only mildly, if at all, for their illegal activities. Socialists heckled, but stormtroopers behind them hissed 'you'll be strung up today'.

The Enabling Law passed by 444 votes against the 94 of the socialists. It ended the rule of law and laid the basis for a new kind of authority based on the will of the Führer. In practice, it licensed the Nazis to act as they saw fit, in the 'higher interests of the German people', against anyone deemed to be an enemy of the Reich. The socialists were the next victims.

Nazism and Fascism

The similarities between the advents to power of Hitler and Mussolini are obvious. We find the same combination of paramilitary terror against the left, deals with conservatives, and reassurances that parliamentary government was safe. Although before they came to power, the Nazis were far less violent than the Fascists had been, they proved incalculably more violent afterwards (see Figure 3).

The question of whether or not Nazism was a form of Fascism remains as impossible as ever because the answer depends on

3. Hitler and Mussolini caught on camera at the Tomb of Fascist Martyrs, Florence, 10 October 1938

definition. The Nazi drive for racial purity can't be explained by a concept that stresses similarities with Fascism. Yet the resemblances between Nazism and Fascism require explanation. They derive from the fact that economic and social structures and ideas cross national boundaries, and consequently, politicians in different countries responded to similar problems in similar ways. Since the experience of total war was transnational, it is no surprise that afterwards paramilitary, nationalist, antisocialist groups emerged quite independently in different states. Subsequently, international exchanges of ideas and policies, through visits, newspaper reporting, and translations, were continuous. Mussolini's seizure of power quickly turned Fascism into an achievement to be emulated.

None of the imitators of Fascism were identical to the original, but national difference was quite compatible with transnational regularities. For one thing, a major purpose of the movements in question was to capture power in territorially bounded states, competing with other nationally focused movements. The rules of politics varied from nation to nation—for instance, Italy was a constitutional monarchy based on male suffrage while Germany was a republic in which women voted—and so the positioning of political parties differed too. For another, many fascists *believed*, albeit with many reservations, that nation was (or, rather, ought to be) the primary form of social solidarity. They thus endeavoured to present themselves as 'national' even when their ideas were actually recycled from diverse sources. We shall see also that there was as much rivalry as emulation between Nazis and Fascists.

The rise to power

The overthrow of the monarchy in the midst of defeat and the establishment of the Weimar Republic were part of a huge upsurge of political and social mobilization. Within it were some groups that resembled Fascism, but which had emerged independently. They included the Freikorps in Germany, which assembled demobilized veterans to fight Socialists, Communists, Poles, and other nationalities. In March 1920, the Pan-German Wolfgang Kapp led the Freikorps Marinebrigade Ehrhardt into Berlin to carry out a coup. The Nazis later claimed the Freikorps as an inspiration. There are obvious similarities to Fascism in their violent anticommunism, and to Nazism in that they kept alive the idea of German rights to territory in Eastern Europe. Yet the Freikorps lacked a syndicalist and trade-union wing and antisemitism was far more important to them than it was to the Italian Fascists. The Freikorps hesitated between nostalgia for the monarchy and the conviction that the *völk* represented the nation.

At that time, Adolf Hitler, a decorated war veteran of Austrian origin, was a member of the German Workers' Party, an insignificant group based in Munich. He soon gained a reputation as the party's best public speaker, and by 1921 he was the absolute leader of the renamed National Socialist German Workers' Party

(NSDAP). The origins of the leader cult may be found in German traditions, such as the aforementioned idea of the 'people's Kaiser', but the Bavarian press also announced Hitler as Germany's Mussolini. In 1923, Hitler cited the Duce as a precedent for his attempted Beer Hall Putsch (in which he co-operated with the Great War general, Eric Ludendorff).

In prison, Hitler set out his ideas in the autobiographical *Mein Kampf*. Germany's mission, he believed, was the conquest of living space in the East, at the expense of 'Judeo-Bolshevik' Russia. Achievement of this goal depended on overcoming German decadence by eradicating democracy and racial enemies. Living space would provide the resources needed to unite the people in a racially pure nation. Domestic and foreign policy objectives were mutually dependent.

These ideas recalled the Wagnerian strand in European culture and 19th-century Social Darwinist, imperialist, and racist ideas that had passed for science in certain university faculties and professions, where they informed projects for engineering a strong society. The Nazis also borrowed aspects of Italian Fascism, including the 'Hitler greeting', which was useful because it reinforced Hitler's authority in the Nazi movement. For the same purpose, Hitler kept a bust of Mussolini in his office.

That Hitler found the road to power longer than Mussolini did warns against seeing Nazism simply as a product of crisis and the 'disorientation' of the population. The upheaval that followed the Great War was at least as serious in Germany as in Italy. Outrage at Germany's treatment at Versailles extended well outside the constituency of the extreme right, as did the conviction that a Socialist 'stab in the back' was responsible for the defeat. The Socialist agitation and electoral gains of 1919 intensified bitterness. Yet the Weimar Republic survived, for key political groups supported it. Unlike their Italian counterparts, German socialists defended the regime, and a general strike ensured

Kapp's failure. The army, the support of which was essential for success, knew that Britain and France would not tolerate a nationalist regime in Germany, so it accepted democracy for the moment.

During the 1920s, the Weimar Republic was relatively stable. The economic situation improved, to some extent. Centrist coalitions managed, just about, to impose coherent government. Rapprochement with France and Britain held out some hope that Germany might recover its eastern territories. Political violence almost subsided. Yet the Communist Party (KPD) never accepted the 'bourgeois republic', while the Nationalist DNVP remained monarchist. The paramilitary veterans' association, the Stahlhelm, was strongly entrenched in Protestant, bourgeois provincial society, and nourished hostility to the Social Democrats, Communists, and the established right. Many of those who would vote Nazi in the 1930s had already espoused populist ultranationalist politics in the previous decade.

These voters condemned the alleged subservience of the Republic to selfish economic interests and demanded a more 'national' policy, while paradoxically demanding defence of their own interests. Weimar politics degenerated into a free-for-all, in which each interest group accused others of refusing to put the national interest (i.e. their own) first. The Nazis triumphed because they convinced wide sections of the electorate that they could subordinate special interests to the nation.

The American crash in 1929 had a grave impact on Germany's fragile society. The slump led to business collapses, indebtedness for farmers, and massive unemployment. The Republic lost whatever legitimacy it had possessed as conservatives felt unable to tolerate its alleged favouritism towards workers, feminists, and Jews. Many of the six million unemployed abandoned for Communism (or in some cases for the Brownshirts) a regime that seemed to have brought misery. Communists gained votes along with the Nazis. Parliamentary rule was impossible, and from 1930, governments had to act by decree. The army, no longer fearful of the Allies, intervened regularly in politics. German democracy was moribund well before Hitler seized power.

In prison for his part in the 1923 putsch, Hitler rethought the Italian example in the light of his own failure and concluded that he could only win power through the ballot box. Electoral propaganda was at first directed primarily at industrial workers, in the hope of detaching them from the KPD. But the 1928 elections showed unexpected gains amongst the Protestant peasantry, who had suffered badly from the agricultural crisis. From then on Nazi propaganda was more targeted at conservative voters, and this paid off with electoral breakthrough in 1930. Once Nazism became a mass force, Mussolini began to take notice, and his personal envoy in Rome advised Hitler on strategy. In any case, Hitler had recognized that Mussolini owed his success to a combination of elections and threats.

That said, the Nazi campaign of intimidation against Socialists, Communists, and Catholics was nothing like that of the Blackshirts in Italy, where many more had died. The Nazis were more than willing to brawl, but their parades were mostly symbolic displays, which presented them as the only force that was disciplined enough to restore order. The Nazis simultaneously adopted an anti-establishment stance, portraying themselves as the real representatives of the people, and denouncing conservative governments as weak and unrepresentative.

Although this populist message was particularly attractive to ex-conservatives, the Nazi vote was broader than that of other parties. The movement won a significant minority of votes from the socialists. It appealed more or less equally to men and women. Around a quarter of the German working class, especially in small firms in small towns, may have voted Nazi in July 1932.

Despite the relative breadth of their appeal, the Nazis, with 37 per cent of the vote in July 1932, didn't have enough seats in parliament to govern. In a new election in November, they lost two million votes. Moreover, although conservative politicians, like the business, military, and land-owning elites, were hostile to the Republic, they distrusted the Nazis as 'brown Bolsheviks', and preferred an authoritarian government run by themselves. The problem was that the elites, rightly or wrongly, felt that no government could survive without mass support. This conviction testified to the extent to which 'democratic' assumptions had penetrated even the reactionary right. It also reflected the army's fear that it couldn't maintain order against both Communists and Nazis. For want of alternatives, the conservatives made Hitler chancellor on 30 January 1933. Like Mussolini, Hitler alone bridged the gap between parliamentary and street politics.

Dictatorship

Besides Hitler, the Nazis only had two representatives in the cabinet. But control over the police, coupled with government by decree, permitted them to unleash a wave of repression against the left. The Reichstag fire served as a pretext to suspend freedom of the press and association. In the elections of 5 March, the Nazis did not do quite as well as expected, but with DNVP support they were able to pass the Enabling Act. In subsequent weeks, trade unions were banned, non-Nazi right-wing parties dissolved themselves, and Jews were removed from state employment. Ordinary people well knew the fate of those who expressed dissent, a fact that should qualify the view that Germans uniformly consented to Nazi rule or simply worshipped Hitler in mass rallies.

Within the regime, several factions jostled for power and were quite prepared to employ violence against each other. The Brownshirts, the Sturmabteilung (SA), which had led the campaign against the left, demanded a second revolution.

The army feared that the SA wished to usurp its position. Partly because of conservative pressure Hitler arrested and executed the SA's leadership on 30 June 1934—the 'night of the long knives'. That did not permit conservatives to regain all their lost ground. Repression was carried out by the Schutzstaffel (SS), which had begun as an elite protection unit, and subsequently took on political responsibilities. Soon after the night of the long knives, the army swore an oath of loyalty to Hitler.

Nazi radicalism was especially evident in the political sphere. The destruction of the rule of law meant not only arbitrary beatings, imprisonment in concentration camps, or execution, but the erosion of the very basis of rule-based government, justice, and administration. The civil service was purged, and the institutions of the Party and SS became parallel administration, the personnel of which was recruited on the basis of ideology and service to the Party, rather than the procedures of the civil service. People of unconventional backgrounds rose into positions of influence. This was not revolution as Marxists understood it, but it destabilized existing power structures.

As with Fascism in Italy, trade-union radicals and those who hoped that Nazism would make women more equal were largely disappointed by Nazism in power (see Chapters 9 and 10). Nonetheless, the Nazis were more successful in ensuring that their dogma penetrated all spheres of society. Previously independent associations, from women's groups to film societies, were dissolved or incorporated into Nazi organizations. School syllabuses were reformed. The workers' leisure organization, the sinisterly named Strength Through Joy, and the German Labour Front, a manifestation of the Nazis' corporatist schemes, were both involved in engineering the Nazi Utopia. Moreover, social policies provided a forum for Fascists and Nazis to exchange expertise.

More than in Italy, the guiding principle of Nazi action was race. Although biological antisemitism was not shared by all Germans or even by all Nazis, a movement had seized power in which biological racism emphatically was an article of faith for many activists and especially leaders. Hitler's enormous popularity, earned by crushing Communism and restoring Germany's international position, coupled with indifference to the fate of the Jews in many quarters, provided antisemites with the opportunity to implement their designs. Racial considerations suffused all policies, from the protection of mothers and the distribution of medical care to diplomacy and educational syllabuses. Furthermore, Nazi racial policies could not have been implemented without the assistance of non-Nazi institutions, especially the army, civil service, and academics.

Indeed, as in Italy, big business, the army, and administration retained some independence, and there was much competition between them and the agencies of party and security services. Yet the balance of power was different in Germany. Business lost its ability to influence government policy collectively as it became increasingly subject to regulation. In 1938, many generals were dismissed and Hitler became commander-in-chief. The SS, under Heinrich Himmler, established its own military force and extended its reach into all areas of racial policy— since racial policy was so important, the power of the SS was enormous. Since the German army, civil service, and professoriate were more open to the Nazi message than their Italian counterparts were to Fascism, the various components of the regime outdid each other in their endeavours to realize Hitler's agenda—they worked, as one activist put it, 'towards the Führer'. There was no need for Hitler to dictate detailed policy—in any case, he had neither the energy nor the aptitude to do so.

The confusion of powers liberated policy-makers from the constraints of morality and law. It made uncertainty a principle of government and reduced the regime's victims to helplessness. The regime's aspiration to totalitarian control was not realized, and there is much evidence of scepticism towards aspects of Nazi rule. But collective resistance was extremely risky, and the regime also offered advantages to members of the favoured ethnic group, such as the promise, if not yet the reality, of a consumer and leisure society.

Like Mussolini, Hitler was passionately interested in diplomacy. He had always regarded the acquisition of *lebensraum* and the elimination of race enemies and Bolshevism as essential to the establishment of a harmonious German society. Hitler did not have a clear idea of how he would achieve these aims, but he did set about preparing Germany for racial war. Most domestic policy was related in one way or another to this priority. Measures to encourage women to marry and bear children were intended to increase the size of the 'healthy' population and provide future soldiers. Sterilization of the 'unfit' would improve the quality of the population. Public works projects had a military dimension; the Four Year Plan of 1936 emphasized arms production and import substitution. It was no accident that the radicalization of Jewish policy in November 1938 followed a war scare. Removal of Jewish influence—extermination was not yet Nazi policy—was seen by the Nazis both as the goal of war and the precondition of success.

Hitler's diplomacy was not guided by a medium-term plan. His hope that Britain might remain neutral and leave Germany free to dominate the Continent was soon disappointed. In 1936, however, Hitler told his generals that a war for living space must take place by 1940 at the latest, and in the following years he seized whatever opportunities came his way. He annexed Austria to the Reich in March 1938, and in September turned his attention to the Sudeten German minority in Czechoslovakia. War finally broke out with Britain and France in September 1939 when Hitler, reassured by alliance with the Soviet Union, invaded Poland. Almost as soon as France had been defeated in 1940, Hitler began to plan an invasion of the Soviet Union.

The invasion unleashed a conflict of unprecedented barbarity. The total destruction of indigenous authority in the conquered eastern lands and the absence of constraints within Germany permitted Nazi organizations to murder, torture, exploit, plunder, and experiment upon defeated populations in line with Hitler's apocalyptic prophesies. Even before war began, Hitler had declared that war would end with the annihilation of European Jewry, and so it turned out. Hitler's fantastic delusions survived the complete collapse of German armies. In his Berlin bunker, he and Goebbels read tarot cards and looked to Frederick the Great for inspiration. His last testament blamed the German people for failing him.

Chapter 5
The diffusion of fascism

Turnu Severin, Romania, May 1924

Despite the weight of evidence against him, Corneliu Codreanu wasn't especially worried as he awaited the verdict in his trial for murder (see Figure 4). Doubtless, the 24-year-old law student at Iaşi University was reassured that the jurors all sported swastika badges, and that even the prosecuting lawyer had mentioned extenuating circumstances: 'Anarchy had penetrated the university because of the large number of foreigners', he said, and appealed for 'Romania for the Romanians'.

Romania had been rewarded for its part in the Allied victory in the Great War with lands carved from the Austro-Hungarian and Russian empires (see Map 2). The population of the 'new territories' included Jewish, Hungarian, and German minorities, which were especially numerous amongst the business and professional classes. Romanians agreed that the 'new territories' must be 'assimilated' into a homogeneous national state or, in the case of the Jews, excluded.

Students like Codreanu were at the forefront of the struggle to 'Romanianize' the new territories, for intellectuals had traditionally seen themselves as the nationalist vanguard. Romania's future lawyers and doctors held Jews responsible for

4. Codreanu inspects his Legionnaires. Note the peasant costume underneath his city overcoat and hat

the brief upsurge of left-wing activity that had followed the Great War and for their own poor career prospects. In 1922, a campaign for the restriction of Jewish enrolment in universities erupted across Romania. Codreanu and his ilk saw the government's opposition to the proposal as evidence of sympathy for Romania's enemies.

In October 1925, Codreanu murdered the Iași prefect of police, an opponent of the student movement. A first attempt to try Codreanu in the Moldovan town of Focșiani was abandoned because of antisemitic riots. In May, the trial reconvened in the small town of Turnu Severin on the distant Danube, which the government hoped would be quieter. Yet thousands of Codreanu supporters stirred up antisemitism. The whole town wore national colours, and many wore swastikas. The Romanian Bar Association tried to ensure that none of its members represented the victim's widow. The prosecution secured the services of a weak counsel, but nonetheless Codreanu was acquitted—to no one's surprise.

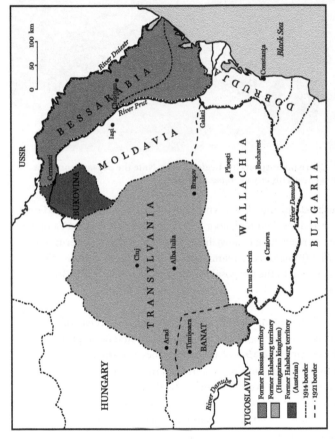

Map 2. Romania

Codreanu was leader of the Legion of the Archangel Michael, best known as the Iron Guard. This organization fought a bitter battle, punctuated by political murders, against a succession of constitutional governments, and then against a royal dictatorship. In November 1938, the latter suppressed the Iron Guard and garrotted Codreanu.

Resemblance of the Iron Guard to Fascism and Nazism is obvious. However, this was no case of simple imitation. The swastika had long been circulating among European far-right groups and its adoption owed nothing to the influence of the still obscure Nazis. In the 1920s, the Iron Guard counted among the admirers of Mussolini, but it also drew from the French neo-royalist movement Action française (AF), in which Romanian émigrés in Paris were active. The Iron Guard shared AF's antisemitism, and in the 1930s that facilitated transfer of allegiance to Nazism.

Entanglements

In the 1920s and 1930s, movements calling themselves 'fascist' or 'national socialist', or claiming inspiration from one or both, appeared all over Europe, the Americas, and in colonized countries. Few parts of the globe were entirely immune from the appeal of fascism, even less so because Hitler and Mussolini actively promoted their ideologies abroad. Many observers believed that the German and Italian regimes offered something new and different, but they did not agree on what that was. Sometimes they categorized these regimes with others, from Stalin's Communism to Kemal Ataturk's socialist nationalism.

Foreign movements interpreted fascism according to their own lights and purposes, borrowed some features, modified others, and did not use some aspects at all. The German and Italian regimes' aggressive nationalism caused problems even for their most fervent foreign admirers, for they too were often jealous of national independence.

Moreover, Fascism and Nazism spread their ideologies not just to fight communism but also to compete with each other, and as the projection outwards of conflicts within each regime. We saw that Hitler initially took Mussolini as a model, and that when Hitler broke through electorally, Mussolini began to see a Nazi government as a potential ally. Once Hitler was in power, Fascists could not decide whether he was a dangerous rival or a comrade. Nazis either admired Fascism or saw Italians as racially inferior.

In 1932–4, some Italian Fascists promoted 'universal fascism', their initiatives culminating in conferences of European movements at Montreux in 1934 and Amsterdam in 1935. They saw this project as a way of reinvigorating Fascism, and as an alternative to Nazi racism. They depicted Fascism as the reincarnation of universal Roman values. That notion resonated with the Iron Guard because Romanian nationalists saw themselves as the heir of classical antiquity (an idea that actually owed much to AF). However, the Fascist International proved unable to match the appeal of Nazism and antisemitism. Even in Italy, some activists saw alignment with Nazism as a more effective means to renew Fascism.

Soon, pro-Nazis gained the upper hand in Italy. Mussolini, in public at least, spoke of aligning the two regimes. In 1936, Germany and Italy signed the Axis alliance, and cooperated in supporting the Nationalists in the Spanish Civil War—a cause that attracted fascists from all over Europe. In 1938, Italy introduced antisemitic legislation. Still, collaboration between Fascism and Nazism was compatible with competition for the allegiance of movements in other countries—and with rivalry on the football field.

Another complicating factor was that fascist influence spread well beyond those who used the label. Some movements, which to other eyes looked similar to fascism, fiercely denied any affinity. Also, the interwar years in Europe witnessed the establishment of dictatorships in country after country, and they too borrowed selectively from fascism.

How many individuals, movements, and regimes we categorize as 'fascist' depends on definition. If we define fascism simply as a desire to manipulate the mass, or as dictatorship, then a great many would qualify. If we add the criteria of racism and/or antisemitism, a different set would be included. The impossibility of agreeing on a definition means that attempts to identify 'true fascism' can never be decisive. However, this difficulty does not prevent us from examining similarities and differences between various movements or actual interactions and borrowings—'entanglements', as scholars call them. I shall ask how and for what purposes the terms 'fascist' and 'national socialist' were used. Tracing entanglements allows us to see that relations of fascists were strongest with conservative groups, dictatorial or parliamentarian (although we shall see in Chapters 8–10 that relations between fascism and the left were not simply oppositional).

Fascists and conservatives in interwar Europe

The concept of totalitarianism makes an absolute distinction between conservatism, parliamentary or dictatorial, and fascism. The former involves government by church, civil service, army, and perhaps monarchy, and it defends family and property. Fascism, in contrast, represents the advent of a new elite, drawn from the people, at the head of a mass party; it threatens the institutions that conservatives hold dear, and it has more in common with communism. Marxists counter that fascists and conservatives shared enemies, and they emphasize the cooperation between them (see Figure 5).

There is something in both these views. In recognition of that, Martin Blinkhorn argues that in interwar Europe there was a continuum from authoritarian conservatism to fascism. At one

5. Fascism and authoritarian conservatism: From left to right
Engelbert Dollfuss of Austria, Mussolini and Gyula Gömbös, the
semifascist prime minister of Hungary, in Rome, 17 March 1934. On
the right is the Japanese ambassador to Italy

end were authoritarian conservative regimes based on established
institutions, with minimal fascist tendencies. At the other end
were fascist movements and regimes with minimal conservative
involvement, of which Nazism was the best example. Blinkhorn's
interpretation recognizes entanglements and transfers between
fascism and conservatism but also allows for conflict between and
within each of them.

Blinkhorn's approach is useful so long as we remember that this
is *our* distinction and that it was not necessarily one that the
protagonists made. And when protagonists did use terms such as
radical and conservative, they often meant something different to
us. What matters is how the terms were *used*. When activists
claimed 'Fascism is this' or 'Nazism is that', and accused their
opponents of 'deviations', such as having a 'conservative' or a
'bourgeois spirit', we must ask what they meant. It is impossible

to trace all the pathways through which fascism was diffused, transformed, and used. I shall confine myself to a few examples.

Fascism in the democracies

Although victorious, France suffered gravely from the Great War, and afterwards the upsurge of industrial unrest provoked fear of yet another revolution in a country that had known so many. Initially, conservatives turned to the parliamentary National Bloc, for having been out of power for 40 years (unlike German and Italian counterparts) parliamentary conservatives were untainted by failure. Nevertheless, the Bloc included many far-right elements, with a following among Catholics, aristocrats, students, and the urban and petty bourgeoisie. Politically, these extremists were a hotchpotch, loyal to various nationalist movements and branches of deposed royalty. The strongest element was the royalist AF, which espoused antisemitism, dictatorship, and Catholicism.

Increasingly frustrated with the Bloc's failure to deliver significant change, the far right welcomed Mussolini's advent to power. To avoid the charge of admiring a foreign ideology, it claimed that Mussolini had copied French ideas. It picked those aspects of fascism that it liked best: antisocialism, strong government, and concessions to the Church. It paid relatively little attention to Fascism as a mass movement, and did not always distinguish Fascism from Miguel Primo de Rivera's military dictatorship in Spain (in 1923, Primo cited Mussolini as an inspiration for his seizure of power).

In 1924, the left returned to power, compounding the discredit of the Bloc and provoking a new wave of fear among conservatives, many of whom now turned to new mass movements. The Jeunesses patriotes (JP) clearly owed something to Fascism, for they wore blue raincoats, used the fascist salute, and fought Communists in the streets. Some JP leaders claimed to be fascists, but others were more circumspect. The movement owed as much to the French Bonapartist tradition; many members were Catholics and some were also active in the parliamentary right. From 1926, the JP largely avoided the fascist label, for it needed to differentiate itself from another mass movement, the Faisceau. As its name suggests, the Faisceau saw itself as the French manifestation of international fascism. It too claimed that Mussolini had reworked French doctrines, but interpreted those traditions differently. The Faisceau emphasized corporatism, but was split by controversies about the independence of workers' unions. In the event, these disputes hardly mattered, for the Faisceau had no chance of coming to power. The French far right lacked presence in parliament; it could not prevail through pressure in the streets alone, and so it was possible for a new conservative coalition to defuse the crisis.

The far right revived during the Slump. On 6 February 1934, a massive demonstration in central Paris forced another left-wing government out of power, but again the far right was too weak in parliament to profit. Subsequently, a new league, the Croix de feu, dominated the right, recruiting up to half a million members, and many more after it became a party in 1936. For its enemies, the Croix de feu was the incarnation of fascism, and one can hardly deny the resemblances. It carried out paramilitary-style manoeuvres that recalled those of the Nazis (more than those of the Fascists); it espoused corporatism and antiparliamentarianism, and attacked both the left and the supposedly too-feeble conservatives. The movement admired some aspects of Fascism and Nazism, especially its pronatalist and social programmes, and learned from the way that Mussolini and Hitler had won power. There were also differences: its constitutional proposals were relatively moderate; it did not advocate territorial expansion (but had no intention of giving up the colonies), and it was far less antisemitic than the Nazis (or AF). Croix de feu leaders, with the odd exception, vehemently denied that they were fascist. They did so because using any label other than 'national' threatened to divide the disparate far right. Furthermore, whereas in the 1920s identification with the former ally, Italy, had been possible, Germany was France's hereditary enemy.

Nonetheless, the left depicted the league as Hitler's agent. It was nothing of the sort, but the strategy was effective. Moreover, the left had learned from the Nazi victory in Germany, where Socialists and Communists had hated each other almost as much as they did the Nazis. The French left, united as the Popular Front, fought the Croix de feu in the streets, and designed policies to entice electors away from the far right. The Popular Front won a large majority in the elections of 1936. The Croix de feu submitted tamely to dissolution, but reappeared as the Parti social français (PSF), which slowly shook off its more fascistic characteristics, only to rediscover the advantages of dictatorship when France was occupied by the Germans in 1940.

Fascism made inroads in Britain too. The Empire was threatened by insurgent nationalism; the economy languished throughout the interwar years, while the General Strike of 1926 and the rise of the Labour Party seemed to endanger property. British conservatives admired Mussolini for restoring order and differentiated moderate Fascism from its allegedly more dangerous radical variety. Some Catholics saw Mussolini as leading the fight against atheistic communism and some intellectuals appreciated the regime's aesthetic modernism. Few thought that Fascism could be transferred to Britain. Those who did formed the British Fascists in 1925. This group did not become a mass movement, but some Conservative Party MPs used it to police meetings.

Only the British Union of Fascists (BUF), founded in 1932 by Sir Oswald Mosley, really mattered, and only briefly. Initially, the BUF was close to Italian Fascism, from which it received funding, but its understanding of Fascism differed from that of the previously mentioned conservatives. Mosley had come from the Labour

Party, and he applauded Fascist corporatism as a more imaginative response to the Depression than that offered by the old parties. Notwithstanding this radicalism, the BUF also owed something to pre-1914 Diehard Toryism, which had opposed the Liberal government's plans for social reform and Irish Home Rule. Some Diehards had anticipated Mosley's promise that the people would soon sweep away the 'old gang'. The BUF itself won support from the Conservative Party, some members of which saw Fascism as legitimating a harder line at a time when Stanley Baldwin had seemingly abandoned conservative principles to join Labour in the National Government (formed in 1929).

Much of the BUF's support evaporated thanks to its violence, and in any case the movement was disadvantaged in Britain's first-past-the-post electoral system. Mosley sacrificed what remained of his chances when he switched his allegiance from Fascism to Nazism (the Italian ambassador transferred his hopes to the Conservative Party). This mistake convinced most Britons that Mosley was a traitor.

In the United States too, those who expressed sympathy for Nazism risked being seen as unpatriotic. The American-German Bund gained no more than 6,000 members at its peak (see Figure 6). It arose partly from indigenous American racism, epitomized by the Ku Klux Klan, which had re-emerged during the War and might have gained 2–8 million members in the 1920s. The Klan anticipated many features of fascism, but also included the anti-state, libertarian, populist individualism that still marks the American extreme right. The Bund was linked to the Klan, but it owed as much to the ill-treatment of Germans, common since America entered the Great War. In the 1930s, Father Charles E. Coughlin's National Union for Social Justice was more successful, but it was less extreme. Coughlin, who had begun as an advocate of Roosevelt's New Deal, preached anticommunism, antisemitism, and anticapitalism. His candidate won 882,479 votes in the 1936 presidential elections.

6. A mass rally of the German-American Volksbund at Madison Square Garden, New York, in February 1939. Note the swastikas superimposed upon the American eagle

The weakness of fascism in the United States warns again against the assumption that crisis breeds extremism automatically. Conditions appeared favourable—for the severity of the economic crisis, conservative dislike of the New Deal, and isolationist opposition to American involvement in the struggle against fascism in Europe—all provided grievances for extremists. The New Deal neutralized discontent, and anti-state individualism took extremists in different directions.

Religion and fascism

Father Coughlin's brew of fascism and Catholicism was not unprecedented, for Catholics the world over were grateful to Mussolini for restoring some of the privileges of the Church and regularizing the Vatican's position in secular Italy. In July 1936, most Catholics also applauded General Francisco Franco's military rising against the Spanish Popular Front government.

However, Spanish Catholics were divided politically and socially. Monarchists and assorted conservatives considered the Republic to emanate from a conspiracy of atheists, Jews, Freemasons, and Marxists, while other Catholics were prepared to accept pluralism within the Republic. Meanwhile, Social Catholics sought to recover the Church's influence through social reform rather than simply repressing enemies. Catholics potentially saw different things in fascism. Some wished simply to destroy the left, but others saw corporatism as a way of reconciling labour and capital. The latter had little influence until the shock of defeat in the elections of February 1936, which prompted more Catholics to look into the reasons for the appeal of socialism. New thinking developed even in the midst of the subsequent Civil War.

The movement that eventually brought Franco to power included a frankly fascist component—the Falange Española, under José Antonio Primo de Rivera, son of the late dictator. Besides imitating Fascist rituals and paramilitary violence, the Falange was officially secular. It appealed nevertheless to Catholics of various stripes. José Antonio insisted that Catholicism was the Spanish national religion. Its admiration for Fascist corporatism converged with Social Catholic thinking about ways to reconcile the classes. It advocated moderate land reform and nationalization of banks. It preached 'national syndicalism', which allegedly differed from Italian corporatism because it was freer of business and state control. In Spain, as elsewhere, it is hard to disentangle the specifically Catholic contribution to corporatism.

The Falange failed to set the tone of Franco's coalition, which also included non-aligned conservatives and people loyal to Spain's rival royal families. Monarchists benefitted from family and class links with the officer corps, which distrusted Falangist radicalism. The army was rendered indispensable by the stubbornness of Republican military defence, while many Falangist activists were killed or imprisoned by the Republicans.

In 1937, the Falange did not resist when Franco incorporated it into a single movement. Like Mussolini's, Franco's regime (which endured until 1975) possessed a single party that included radical fascists as well as conservatives, but contrary to Italian and German developments, the Church, army, and administration strengthened with time.

In Austria, fascism and religion were entangled with the question of union with Germany. Since 1933, an authoritarian government under Engelbert Dollfuss and then Kurt von Schuschnigg, backed by the paramilitary Heimwehr (Home Guard) had governed the country. Mussolini backed this regime because he wanted to preserve his international pre-eminence and did not want to see German expansion towards Italy, where there were Germanophone minorities. To please Mussolini, the Austrian government promised to embrace 'fascism', setting up a corporatist state, the Ständestaat, which also derived from a conservative version of Social Catholicism. As for the 'Austro-fascist' Heimwehr, it wished to revive the supranational Austro-Hungarian Empire, which had collapsed in 1918, in the form of a pro-Mussolini confederation of Catholic states. This supranationalism warns against the assumption that those who called themselves fascists necessarily placed the nation above all other loyalties.

The Heimwehr proved too radical and antisemitic for the leaders of the Ständestaat. In 1936, the government dissolved it and incorporated its followers into its own regime party. Some Heimwehr activists joined the most dangerous enemy of the regime, the Austrian branch of the Nazi Party, thus revealing that Nazism could be attractive to Catholics too. The Austro-Nazis had already attempted a coup in 1934. Then, Mussolini had saved the regime, but once he had joined the Axis, Austria's days as an independent state were numbered. In 1938, Hitler invaded Austria and overthrew the Ständestaat on the grounds that it was 'reactionary'.

Eastern Europe

The new democracies of Eastern Europe, created in a wave of optimism out of the ruins of the multinational Russian, German, and Austro-Hungarian empires, toppled like ninepins during the interwar years. Czechoslovakia alone avoided a *coup d'état*, only to fall into the Nazis' clutches in 1938–9. The apprentice democracies suffered all of the problems of Italy and Germany—wartime destruction, popular unrest, strikes, economic difficulties, and ethnic tensions. There was the same pervasive fear of Bolshevism, exacerbated in some cases by actual war with the Bolsheviks. The Soviet Union had territorial claims on many Eastern European states, and there was a rash of communist insurrections. Communists exploited the grievances of the working class, of peasants (who wanted more land), and of ethnic minorities. There was the same conviction that the war had upset the normal balance between the sexes. As in Italy and Germany, nationalists called for tougher measures against communists, feminists, and ethnic minorities, all in the name of national unity.

This was a powerful message in the ethnic maelstrom of interwar Eastern Europe. The peace treaties had supposedly been based on national self-determination. But intermixing of ethnic groups was so complex that it was impossible to make international frontiers coincide with them. Some frontiers were settled by force. The new 'national' states all included substantial ethnic minorities— Poland, for instance, was only 70 per cent Polish. Formerly subject nationalities became masters of new minorities. Initially governments were relatively tolerant, for peace treaties required protection of minority rights. However, Germany, Bulgaria, Austria, and Hungary resented having lost territory in the peace treaties and were sensitive to the fortunes of fellow nationals who had been reduced to minority status in other states—Hungarians in Romania or Germans in Poland, for instance. Those states that had gained through expansion (Romania and Yugoslavia) or had been newly created (Estonia, Latvia, Lithuania, Czechoslovakia) wanted to 'nationalize' or exclude minorities. In Eastern Europe, as in the West, democracy often meant dictatorship of the majority, not toleration, and still less multiculturalism.

We must be cautious, however, for significant fascist movements did not emerge in all those countries in which circumstances were apparently favourable. In multinational Czechoslovakia and Yugoslavia, fascist movements did not develop among dominant Czech or Serb nationalities, even though some saw their governments as too attentive to ethnic minorities, and both countries experienced economic problems and left-wing agitation. In Czechoslovakia, there was no political space for fascism, for socialism monopolized working-class votes, and the government had used price support to appease farmers. While Czech nationalism possessed blind spots, Czechs prided themselves on being more tolerant and enlightened than their former German rulers. Indeed, Nazism developed among the German minority in the Sudeten region, which increasingly favoured union with Germany.

Elsewhere in Europe, in state after state, conservatives installed authoritarian regimes that repudiated minority-rights treaties, arrested communists, and declared their intention to return women to the home. The left often identified these regimes with fascism, and they did borrow from the Italian and German regimes. Whether that qualifies them as fascist is a matter of definition, but what is certain is that they combined Fascist precedents with rule through established institutions, and that did not wholly differentiate them from Fascism or Nazism. In Romania, Orthodox Primate Miron Cristea became prime minister in 1938. The army became the mainstay of government in Poland. The army and landed magnates were preponderant in Hungary. In Bulgaria, Romania, and Yugoslavia monarchies governed directly. Everywhere civil servants were influential.

Elitist as they were, some dictatorships created mass parties. In 1935, the Polish 'colonels' set up the Camp of National Unity, while the Yugoslav Radical Union was designed to provide popular support for a royal dictatorship—members wore green shirts. The Yugoslav regime also accepted support from the Yugoslav Women's Union, seeing its educational and welfare activities as a means to encourage loyalty to the monarchy. These groups, a new feature of European conservatism, both imitated and competed with fascists, but also deferred to the established authorities, and had no organizational monopoly. Indeed, most of these dictatorships tolerated some political freedoms. Censorship was incomplete; the opposition was subject to arrest and imprisonment, but continued to exist. Constitutions were modified and ballots were manipulated, but elections were still held. In general, the law was still observed, albeit a markedly authoritarian law.

Fascists, who were torn between opposition to and collaboration with these dictatorships, were most successful in Hungary and Romania. The former was ruled from 1919–44 by Admiral Miklós Horthy, who headed a semi-authoritarian conservative regime, which shaded into the fascist opposition. The latter was unusual for two reasons. First, besides admiring Mussolini, the Hungarian extreme right established links with Hitler before 1923, attracted by the German movement's extreme hostility to the peace treaties and by its antisemitism—for Jewish universalism was said to have undermined the ethnic Hungarian nation. This message resonated with the officer class and bureaucrats who had recently governed a great empire; they felt national humiliation keenly and resented Jewish competition for jobs. The second unusual feature was social radicalism: fascists demanded the breakup of Hungary's great estates, the power base of the regime.

In 1932, Horthy made the fascist Gyula Gömbös prime minister on condition that he renounced antisemitism. Gömbös duly aligned himself with Mussolini, whom he had long admired anyway, but returned to Hitler after 1933, attracted by the promise of treaty revision and by German economic power. Nevertheless, Gömbös found himself hemmed in by Conservative opponents. He achieved little, and that left space for pro-Nazi groups, of which the Arrow Cross was most important. The Arrow Cross was not ultranationalist. It hesitated between religious and racial underpinnings for Hungarian nationalism, and claimed not to be chauvinist. Indeed, it coupled antisemitism with criticism of Nazism for using the 'Jewish' idea of the chosen people. It preferred a confederation of southeastern states like that advocated by Austro-Fascists. The movement's antisemitism resonated with urban workers, whose employers were often Jewish. Gömbös's government achieved mixed results, for he faced resistance within the government from conservatives, and his death in 1936 shifted the initiative back to the latter. In 1939, Horthy moved against the Arrow Cross, but could not prevent it doing well in the 1939 elections. Anyway, Horthy's own regime countered the 'extremists' by becoming ever more dictatorial and antisemitic, and it opposed Arrow Cross partly for its plan to grant autonomy to ethnic minorities. Hungary joined Hitler's wars of aggression and carried out violence against minorities in recovered territories, including Romania. It was hard to see where fascism began and ended.

Returning briefly to Romania, it too was ruled after 1920 by authoritarian 'liberal' governments and then from 1928 by a monarchical regime. Codreanu's Iron Guard provided the main opposition, and charged the government with being insufficiently committed to Romanianization of this ethnically diverse country. The Iron Guard is noteworthy also because it resembled a 'political religion'. Codreanu saw Romanian Orthodoxy as coterminous with Romanian nationality, so Jews were excluded from the nation both as an urban people and on religious grounds. Yet the Iron Guard was loyal to Orthodoxy in the way that a heretical sect might have been. Codreanu opposed the right of the Church to govern political behaviour. He coupled Orthodoxy to the romantic myth of Romanian rebirth, and evoked the advent of a 'new man'. The Iron Guard displayed its religiosity through bizarre rituals that grotesquely mimicked those of organized religion—members of the Legion's death squads ritually drank each other's blood. This religion divided the world into good and evil. It made politics the domain of struggle and war, and the Legion was an extremely violent organization. Members' willingness to fight to the death was matched only in the SS, in which occult ideas were also present. However, the religiosity of the Iron Guard does not make it a political religion in the sense theorists of that concept understand it, for the members of the Iron Guard did not surrender to blind irrationality. Rituals had the rational purpose of binding the organization together; violence was targeted at specific groups, and enmities were inseparable from quite specific concerns, such as competition for professional employment and peasant desire for land.

The Legion's belief that the nation was to be embodied in the people rather than in the dynasty did not render it popular with the church hierarchy or the monarchy, which soon began to treat the Legion as an enemy. In 1937, the king formed a dictatorial government under Miron Cristea. In 1938, the Legion was banned, and Codreanu was killed.

The Legion re-emerged in 1940, for the defeat of France destroyed the morale of the traditionally Francophile conservative government. Also in 1940 Hitler awarded large tracts of Romanian territory to Hungary and Bulgaria (Stalin helped himself to Bessarabia). The king was blamed for the destruction of the nation, and the Legion was vindicated. Under the conservative General Antonescu the Legion was incorporated into government. However, Antonescu believed the Legion's confiscation of the businesses, farms, and homes of Jews and other minorities went too far. In January 1941, Antonescu won a trial of strength because the Nazis saw him as a more reliable ally than the ultranationalist Legion. Antonescu ensured that Romania participated in the invasion of the Soviet Union, through which he hoped to expand national territory.

Fascism outside Europe

Before 1945, hardly anywhere in the world was untouched by fascism. Anticolonial nationalists could not help but be interested in regimes that threatened colonial rulers and seemed to offer an ideology of national construction. Yet as in Europe, racism and expansionism were major obstacles to the diffusion of fascism, and anyway nationalist movements often sympathized with European antifascists.

In Egypt and Syria, a certain vogue for fascism challenged the dominant liberal-nationalist elites. The economic crisis of the 1930s discredited the liberal-nationalist expectation that the spread of parliamentary self-government on the Anglo-French models would bring them independence. Some young officers and administrators saw in fascism an efficient and dynamic alternative. The Italian regime, meanwhile, posed as the defender of Islam; it built mosques, promoted the use of Arabic, and presented its invasion of Ethiopia as an attack on the Christian enemies of Islam. Paramilitary youth movements using fascist regalia and rituals appeared in Egypt and Syria.

The fascist wave did not last. Other nationalists were convinced that Italian propaganda covered imperial ambitions. Anyway, Islam did not necessarily regard Ethiopia negatively, for the country had sheltered the Prophet in his early days. Political Islam, notably the Muslim Brotherhood, was not interested in fascism at all, while parliamentary nationalism resisted well, and indeed became strongly antifascist. In Palestine, Fascism faced competition from Germany, which attempted a fusion of Islam with Nazism, drawing selectively from radical Christian and Islamic traditions, notably emphasizing antisemitism and hostility to democracy.

In India, a left-leaning leader of the Congress Party, Subhas Chandra Bose, was initially attracted to Fascism as the heir of the

19th-century Italian national revival, the Risorgimento. In 1926, he claimed that India would realize a new synthesis of fascism and communism, and for obvious reasons the British depicted him as a fascist. Under pressure from antifascists in Congress, Bose moderated his views, partly also because Hitler justified British rule in India on racial grounds. Bose looked instead to the socialist authoritarianism of Kemal Attaturk. But he never abandoned hope that Britain's enemies would help India achieve independence. In 1941, he escaped to Berlin, where he helped to form an Indian Legion recruited from POWs, before transferring his hopes to the Indian National Army, formed from Japan's POWs.

Fascism had some appeal in semi-independent non-European states too. In China, the Blueshirts hoped that fascism would revitalize the Kuomintang nationalist movement, but they were more of a secret society than a mass, paramilitary movement. In 1932, Chaing Kai Sheck co-opted them in his bid to return to leadership of the Kuomintang, following a brief withdrawal. Back in power, he used fascist precedents to reform the regime, but combined them with Confucian strictures concerning moral behaviour.

Recourse to dictatorship was frequent in Latin America, and there too some movements and regimes admired fascism. Usually, they looked to the authoritarian aspects of Fascism; mass fascism rarely flourished because levels of political mobilization in these poor societies were low. Neither had Latin America experienced anything like the Great War and its consequent brutalization and militarization of politics. With army backing, governments could easily suppress popular opposition. In any case, there was no left to speak of in most countries. The very familiarity of dictatorship meant that a potential Mussolini would have struggled to distinguish himself from the run-of-the-mill macho military ruler and acquire the aura of a saviour.

Brazil was one exception. Getúlio Vargas's overthrow of the liberal and oligarchic 'Old Republic' in 1930 occurred at a time of crisis caused by the collapse of prices for coffee, Brazil's main source of income. The ensuing economic and social dislocation provoked polarization between communists and the fascistic Integralists. The latter, with at least 200,000 members, rejected liberalism in favour of nationalism, antisemitism, and anticommunism. They sought to weld the country's diverse ethnicities into a Brazilian race defined in historical and cultural terms and to replace a system based on patronage with one of loyalty to nation and regime. They dreamed of the mobilized nation and adopted the usual rituals, salutes, and shirts (green). As always, it's hard to disentangle fascist influence from religion and also in this case from a military reform movement (the tenentes). Moreover, Fascist and Nazi regimes competed for influence over the Integralists, through the medium of Italian and German immigrants.

As in Romania and Hungary, the Integralists came into conflict with an increasingly dictatorial regime. In 1937, Vargas established the authoritarian 'New State', in alliance with the coffee-planter elite and sections of the urban middle classes. He dissolved the Integralists on the pretext of subservience to foreign powers. Interestingly, the regime took a much harder line against pro-Nazis, for the Italians' claim of Latin solidarity had some resonance in Brazil. Vargas's dictatorship imitated some aspects of the authoritarian and Catholic strand of Fascism. The Integralists had been unable to establish a party broad enough to compete with Vargas's manipulation of patronage. Neither were they able to match the Eastern European fascists' appeal to the rural poor, who remained in thrall to planters.

The Latin American regime that most resembled fascism was Juan Domingo Perón's dictatorship in Argentina. The country was more industrialized than most Latin American states and had a long tradition of radical rightism, indebted to the conservative

Catholic nationalism of France and Spain. In 1943, Perón began as labour minister in the military government that had been established in 1943. In a bid to provide the regime with popular support, Perón turned to the trade unions. He negotiated a deal, according to which the government introduced welfare and income redistribution, while the unions backed Argentina's bid for international pre-eminence. In 1946, following the fall of the military regime, Perón won election to the presidency. His combination of nationalism and socialism, coupled with admiration for Mussolini, and the attempt to organize a single party, rightly caused observers to see parallels with fascism. Yet the fact that Perón had not come to power at the head of a mass party meant that Argentina did not witness the undermining of the state structures that happened in Italy and Germany. Perónism also left room for opposition.

The failure of fascist movements

Although many regimes and movements imitated aspects of fascism, explicitly fascist movements generally struggled to become regimes. There is no straightforward reason for this failure, for economic crisis and fear of communism were very widespread, even where actual communists were rare.

The most convincing explanation is that fascism did best where it combined leverage in parliament with street action, as it had in Italy and Germany, and to a lesser extent in Hungary. In Italy and Germany, fascists were strong in both. In Hungary, Gömbös came to power in a parliamentary government, but lacked sufficient power outside to resist conservative coalition partners. In France, the right was weak in parliament. The French far right was generally so antiparliamentarian that it refused to take part in elections; it could not rely on a solid bloc of its own deputies when it came to forming governments, and never converted success on the streets into power. Anyway, the electoral system did not favour extremists in the way that it did in Germany and Italy.

In Eastern Europe and Brazil, fascists did win elections. But in countries with little tradition of democracy, conservatives were quite happy to suspend parliament whenever it looked as if fascists might pose a significant threat. Furthermore, Eastern European fascists were more socially radical than counterparts in Germany or Italy were. Demands for the expropriation of Jewish property, and strikes against 'foreign' employers, looked more dangerous in Eastern Europe, where Jews and other ethnic minorities made up a large proportion of the bourgeoisie. And fascists directly attacked the landowning indigenous elites by supporting peasant demands for land. Antonescu and his ilk disliked movements that had almost as little regard for property as the communists. Lacking conservative support, Eastern European fascists could win power only with support from the Nazis. Because the latter distrusted the fascists' extreme nationalism, that was not always forthcoming.

Chapter 6
Phoenix from the ashes?

> Ur-Fascism [a term meaning 'eternal fascism'] is still around
> us, sometimes in plainclothes. It would be so much easier for
> us if there appeared on the scene somebody saying, 'I want to
> reopen Auschwitz, I want the Blackshirts to parade again
> in the Italian squares'. Life is not that simple. Ur-Fascism can
> come back under the most innocent of disguises. Our duty
> is to uncover it and point the finger at any of its new
> instances—every day and in every part of the world.
>
> Umberto Eco, 22 June 1995

Stirring as Eco's appeal is, it won't do as a way to understand
fascism in contemporary society. If it were possible for fascism to
dress in 'plainclothes', how could we tell which of the myriad
movements around us was fascist? Should we look at those which
most resemble our idea of fascism or those that least resemble it?

Eco breaks a fundamental rule of academic enquiry (and indeed of
any fruitful exchange between people). To be useful, a proposition
must be *falsifiable*—one must be able to imagine evidence that
could in theory refute the statement. No evidence could contradict
Eco's view that a movement was fascist. If one said that such and
such essential characteristic was missing from the movement in
question, the rejoinder would always be 'Ah! but they're in
plainclothes'.

Certainly, we might uncover evidence that far-right leaders, especially when they address purists among their followers, claim their moderate stance is just a cover for fascism, which will be jettisoned in power. Yet leaders alone do not define the nature of a party. If the moderate policy is successful, it will attract more moderate members and voters, and that will constrain the leaders, with unpredictable results. Indeed, in Italy, a moderate strategy ultimately led to incorporation of Italian neo-fascists into mainstream conservatism. In contrast, the moderate strategy of the British National Party (BNP) ultimately caused infighting and that contributed to decline of the party.

Except in Italy, parties that explicitly claim to be Fascist or Nazi have rarely been electorally significant, and so they are not central to this chapter. My concern is rather with those that have enjoyed a degree of success. These parties invariably rejected the fascist label, but their enemies (and more rarely academics) have accused them of fascism. Once again, I shan't attempt to settle the question of whether these parties *were* fascist, for the answer depends on definition. We can only say that there are so many differences between interwar and modern extreme right movements that a definition that included all of them would be very broad.

I shall treat postwar fascism as I did its spread in the first half of the century. On the one hand, I shall elucidate some of the similarities and differences between present-day and interwar movements, without addressing the impossible question of whether or not they are 'fundamentally' the same. On the other hand, I shall examine the perspective of the protagonists, by tracing some of the ways in which these movements understood fascism and the grounds on which they rejected the label.

Fascism's afterlife

In 1945, fascism was deeply discredited, and most postwar regimes in the USSR, Britain, and the USA owed their legitimacy to the struggle against it. In Germany, although opinion polls revealed that many people felt Nazism to have been a good idea badly carried out, neo-Nazis have so far achieved only regional successes. The German constitution forbids the formation of antidemocratic parties, and governments of left and right have been prepared to ban fascist organizations. Throughout the postwar years, the German economic miracle and stable government have ensured that no party was in a position to break this ban. Italian society has been less secure, but when in 1960 a Christian Democrat government used the votes of neo-fascist deputies to remain in office, massive demonstrations forced the prime minister to resign. Fear of foreign criticism obliged even the Franco dictatorship to allow Christian democrats and monarchists to increase their influence at the expense of the Falange.

This is not to deny the existence of a great many movements explicitly inspired by Nazism and Fascism. Sometimes use of the label implied a deliberate attempt to place oneself outside society. An American investigator's conversation with Charles Hall, commander of the White Aryan Legion, revealed something of this psychology.

> You know, a true white separatist—a true National Socialist… always felt the same way. Was always attracted to the swastika, to the iron cross and stuff… The swastika without doubt is the most hated symbol, but it should be the most loved and cherished symbol there is… When you put… a swastika on your skin or you wear it on your shirt, you've separated yourself from 99.9 percent of the population.
>
> (Quoted in Betty E. Dobratz and Stephanie L. Shanks-Meile, *'White Power, White Pride': The White Separatist Movement in the United States*)

Characters such as Hall deliberately reject mainstream politics and society. In the 1990s, there were at most 10,000–20,000 members of the overtly neo-fascist groups in the United States.

These grouplets struggle not only against the opprobrium of fascism, but against the quite different traditions of the American extreme right.

Take, for instance, the Patriot Movement: a hotch-potch of militias that sprouted after the death of 76 people in Waco, Texas, in February 1993, following the FBI's siege of the headquarters of a religious sect. The militias held that the armed citizenry of the American Revolution should prevent the federal government from running amok again. Only the gun-toting citizen could defend the original constitution of the American people against a government bent on selling out the country to the global world order.

The militias share the nationalism, populism, and anticommunism of fascism and the present-day European far right, but they differ in that they are strongly libertarian. They deny the government's right to issue drivers' licences or tax the people. Some claim that the government infringes the true meaning of the constitution; others say that the constitution was imposed upon free Americans, and even that it is a cover for the continued rule of the US by the United Nations, Papacy, British monarchy, or international finance. This hostility to a pro-globalization federal government recalls that of European extremists to the European Union. Some Patriots held that only whites possessed the original American freedoms, which were never intended for blacks.

Turning to Europe, the story of the Italian Social Movement (MSI), shows the disadvantages of using the fascist label, even in relatively favourable terrain. Founded in 1946, the MSI unashamedly assumed Mussolini's mantle and at first was directed by Fascists living clandestinely. It survived largely because Italy did not possess a credible democratic conservative party. Most conservative voters backed the centrist Christian Democrats out of fear that supporting a right-wing party would divide anti-Communist forces. Those conservatives who refused to back the Christian Democrats voted for the MSI or for the equally marginal monarchists.

For a half-century, the MSI wrestled with the contradictions of the fascist heritage, and it included many factions and views on what fascism had been. It drew its social programme—corporatism, workers' participation in management, and some nationalization of key industries—from the radical wing of Fascism. Its political programme was more moderate: a presidential constitution close to the US model. Usually the moderates dominated, and they advocated alliance with conventional conservatives, for the party did best electorally amongst southern conservatives who had rallied to Mussolini after his conquest of power. In the 1960s and 1970s, some frustrated radicals split off and engaged in a campaign of terrorist provocation. Whichever faction was dominant, the MSI never won more than 9 per cent of the vote—usually far less.

In October 1992, the MSI celebrated the seventieth anniversary of the March on Rome with parades, Roman salutes, and songs. That year, however, witnessed a fundamental change in the movement's relationship to Fascism, precipitated by the collapse of communism in Eastern Europe. The powerful Italian Communist Party transformed itself into a social-democratic party, thereby depriving the extreme right of its main enemy. The same year saw the emergence in 1992 of the Northern League under Umberto Bossi, dedicated to winning the autonomy of the allegedly more productive north from the 'African' south, a prospect that caused the largely southern MSI to defend the existing regime. Then, in 1992–3, the hitherto dominant Christian Democrats imploded under the impact of fraud investigations. Antifascism ceased to be the touchstone of political acceptability, and electoral space opened on the right, into which the MSI stepped.

Led by Gianfranco Fini, a new generation of activists without personal links to Fascism transformed the party. Fini made gestures of reconciliation with the antifascist Resistance, repudiated dictatorship, accepted democracy as a system of values, and disavowed Fascist racial legislation. The reformed MSI gave Italy what it had never had—a self-consciously right-wing Catholic conservative party. In 1995, the MSI confirmed these changes by transforming itself into the Alleanza Nationale (AN). A year earlier, the movement had gained 14 per cent of the vote and entered the government of the media mogul Silvio Berlusconi, and participated in all subsequent right-wing governments. In 2009, the AN merged with Berlusconi's People of Freedom Party, although conflict among conservatives continued.

Certainly, the AN was indebted to Fascism—use of the term 'post-fascist' was meant to acknowledge that. The party's radical wing survived several schisms, for instance in 2003 when Alessandra Mussolini, the dictator's granddaughter, left. Some members showed sympathy for the skinhead politics of football hooliganism. The AN cited revolutionaries of left and right as its inspiration—in this case the Communist Antonio Gramsci and Italy's answer to Heinrich Himmler, Julius Evola. While the AN mainstream rejected the idea that races are unequal, it saw immigration as a threat to national identity. To see the AN as fascist, however, requires a very broad definition. In fact, the Italian right's most extreme element is the Northern League, which is obsessed with immigration and believes the EU to be run by paedophiles.

In post-1945 France, it was even more difficult for a movement that aspired to political influence to use the fascist name. Close association with France's indigenous extremist tradition was not advisable either, given its collaborationist past. In 1972, the formation of the National Front (FN) recognized that difficulty. The Front linked several organizations that wanted to exploit immigration as an electoral issue. As leader, they chose Jean-Marie Le Pen. In 1983 the party won 17 per cent of the vote in the municipal elections in Dreux. In spite of schisms, and the succession of Jean-Marie Le Pen by his daughter Marine in 2012, the party has usually scored well over 15 per cent in presidential elections. In 2002, thanks to the division of the left, Jean-Marie Le Pen was second to incumbent President Jacques Chirac, thus earning the right to confront the latter in the run-off ballot.

In some respects, the FN resembles fascism. Whereas Fini made gestures of reconciliation with antifascists, Le Pen aroused suspicions that he sympathized with the 'revisionist' view of the Holocaust (with those who say that it didn't happen). Notwithstanding, the FN has a strong interest in denying any debt to fascism. On foundation, it used the label 'national' as a more acceptable way to unite its disparate followers and appeal broadly, but it faced strong competition from the left, which because of its Resistance inheritance, could also claim to incarnate the nation. In its breakthrough years, when it focused particularly on winning disillusioned conservatives, it claimed to be the 'true right'. In recent years, it has adopted the label 'national-populist', which combined the advantages of the national label with the appearance of expressing ordinary people's disgust with established politicians of left and right.

The Front denies racism, yet advocates the repatriation of immigrants in the name of defence of national identity. Its social policy is summed up in the term 'national preference', which means giving priority in housing, welfare, and education to 'French' people. Like fascists, the FN wavered between free market and corporatist economics, but so did many non-fascist parties.

The FN's clearest divergence from fascism is that it does not categorically oppose democracy. On the contrary, its declared goal is to reinforce the sovereignty of the people by the use of the referendum and the restoration of the powers of parliament (in the Fifth Republic power lies with the executive). These reforms will allegedly loosen the grip on power of unelected technocrats and establishment politicians, and allow the real wishes of the people concerning immigration, the death penalty, and 'national preference' to be heard. Unlike interwar fascists, the FN does not demand an end to competitive elections, and there's no evidence that it intends to establish a dictatorship. Neither has the FN combined electoralism with violence in the way that Mussolini and Hitler did. The FN does not possess a paramilitary wing comparable to those of historic fascists, though it does attract skinheads and others who are prepared to use violence.

The abandonment of paramilitarism is not simply a question of pursuing the same ends through different means. That Hitler's and Mussolini's conquest of power depended on the pressure of their armed followers was crucial for the nature of their regimes. How different would the history of fascism have been if the Blackshirts, SA, and SS had not aspired to take over some of the functions of the civil service, police, and army? Paramilitary groups may not have achieved all their ends, but we would make little sense of fascism in interwar Europe if we regarded their actions as secondary.

The FN might have started from the intention of rendering fascism more acceptable, yet by stripping it of dictatorship, one-party rule, and paramilitarism, it has become something different. In effect, it exploits the too-widespread identification of democracy with the absolute enforcement of the will of the majority, and it separates democracy from pluralism and toleration.

The problem of linking the modern far right to interwar fascism is especially evident in the case of Russia. True, the Black Hundreds had done well before 1914, and in the 1917–18 Civil War, the Whites were part of the Europe-wide counterrevolutionary movement that provided some of the ingredients of fascism. However, the Communist dictatorship subsequently cut Russia off from the development of fascism, and changed the reference points in the political landscape. After the collapse of the Soviet Union, the far right developed as a mutation of communism.

In December 1993, Vladimir Zhirinovsky's absurdly named Liberal Democratic Party (LDP) won around 25 per cent of the party preference votes in elections to the Duma (parliament). The Party was originally founded on the initiative of the Communist Party, in an attempt to use the nationalist, populist, and antisemitic dimensions of Stalinism to appeal to the disadvantaged. The Party soon developed its own momentum. Zhirinovsky himself is a flamboyant character, part showman, part fantasist, part ultranationalist, and part male chauvinist. Casting his vote, he declared 'Political impotence is finished. Today is the beginning of the orgasm. All the people, I promise you, will feel the orgasm of next year's [presidential elections]'. Zhirinovsky's message was simple. The Russian people and the Russian spirit would raise Russia from its knees. He promised restoration of the Russian empire and attacked foreigners and Jews.

Zhirinovsky has remained a presence in Russian politics, but a minority presence, for others have stolen his policies. Among them is the Russian Communist Party under Gennady Zyuganov, reinvented as an ultranationalist movement. Soviet Communism always contained a populist hatred of the rich and foreigners, and Zyuganov admires Lenin and Stalin for having preserved the Russian state in the face of civil war and foreign invasion. Now the Communists dumped 'Western materialist Marxism' in favour of spiritual nationalism, and enthroned the Orthodox Church as the embodiment of Russian history. Zyuganov claimed to speak for the Russian people against foreign-controlled fat cats like Gorbachev and Yeltsin. He boasts of never having had a serious conversation with a woman.

There is certainly much here that resembles Fascism and indeed National Socialism. Yet it remains difficult to advocate a return to dictatorship in Russia. Like Le Pen, Zyuganov is reluctant to break entirely with the market economy or with democracy. He wants to retain the multiparty system, and to increase the powers of parliament, where the National Communists are strong. The

National Communists won (so far as that is possible in Russia's confused political system) the parliamentary elections of December 1995, and Zyuganov has continued to get around 17 per cent in presidential elections—a distant second to Vladimir Putin (or to Putin's surrogate).

Zyuganov continues to attack Putin from the right, but the latter has captured many of the themes of the National Communists since he became prime minister in 1999 and president in 2000. The previously unknown Putin, a former KGB official, won massive popularity by fighting a vicious war against Chechen separatists and by posing as a man of action (proud of his Judo black-belt). Pluralism has not been eradicated, but there is less freedom than there was in the 1990s. The very conservative Orthodox Church possesses considerable influence—it sees homosexuality as a threat to the nation. Far-right violence is relatively tolerated, while democratic protest is restricted. Putin describes himself as 'a democrat—a Russian democrat'.

Explanations

However problematic the relationship between the modern far right and historic fascism is, and however different the movements in question are, we can hardly avoid the fact that many people *believe* that these groups share something fundamental, and that belief is an essential element in political life.

One consequence of this belief is that there are many entanglements between far-right parties. The precedents of the National Front (NF) in Britain and the MSI in Italy influenced the establishment of the French FN. The BNP is linked to avowedly fascist splinter groups that rejected the moderation of the MSI. Delegates from many of these parties have attended European gatherings, and some belong to the same group in the European Parliament. These contacts did not prevent ideological disputes and nationalist rivalries similar to those witnessed before 1945. The Russian LDP formed links with the German far right, but its anti-German nationalism soon soured relations. The Dutch nationalist, Geert Wilders rejects any affinity at all with Le Pen, whom he condems as a fascist.

Given the diversity of the extreme right, there can be no simple explanation for its emergence. Opposition to globalization is an obvious starting point, given that from Manchester to Moscow, the extreme right denounces McDonalds and attacks immigrants. In Western Europe, the far right castigates the European Union (EU) as an agent of globalization, just as Americans attack the UN. The incorporation of the new democracies of Eastern Europe into the EU provokes fear of a new wave of immigration from the East.

It does not follow that because the far right attacks globalization, then globalization is a cause in a simple sense (any more than 'modernization' was an explanation for fascism). The difficulty is that globalization is not a recent phenomenon; nation-states have always had to reckon with the internationalizing tendencies of capitalism, technological change, and advanced communications. Back in the 1880s, the radical right saw the Jewish Rothschild bank as the personification of the occult power of cosmopolitan finance capital. It is more informative to ask why and how the term 'globalization' is mobilized in particular circumstances, for close inspection reveals that people are very selective in what counts as globalization. Politicians periodically invoke it in order to justify their policies ('accept lower wages, or we won't be able to compete internationally and you will lose your job!'). Few people reject globalization entirely. For instance, an independent bookseller in France might resent competition from the global internet sellers, while welcoming income from translations of the Harry Potter books. We must ask which aspects of internationalization the far right attacks and why, and without forgetting that there are also important national barriers to internationalization.

To begin with, antifascism no longer structures the political landscape. Generational turnover rendered the antifascist reference 'mechanical'. The student uprisings of 1968 inadvertently weakened antifascism further, for activists ridiculed what they saw as their elders' cynical manipulation of antifascism to legitimate their power. Students indiscriminately accused contemporary governments of fascism, and helped empty the term of specific content.

Another reason for the greater acceptability of extreme-right politics is that intellectuals have redefined ultranationalism. In effect, they have translated xenophobia and intolerance into liberal-democratic universalist language. They have re-worked liberal values in three sometimes contradictory ways. First, a crucial role was played by the French thinker Alain de Benoist and the 'New Right' of the 1970s. This movement represented a reaction against the student movement of 1968, but it combined traditional sources of right-wing inspiration with certain liberal ideas in an ideology that was designed to subvert universal democratic values. Much of the New Right's output was not new—one has no difficulty in recognizing an updating of the pseudo-science that inspired interwar fascism (the inevitable struggle between nations, the survival of the fittest, the necessary inequality of individuals, the need for racial purity). What was original (or almost so, for the radical Nazi Otto Strasser had espoused similar ideas) was the use of 'equal rights' to justify discrimination against minorities within states. The New Right claimed that to preserve the alleged distinctiveness of a given nation, it was necessary to discriminate against minorities for races had a right to be pure. It was not immediately obvious that this updating of ultranationalism would pay dividends, for the New Right appealed only to a small (but Europe-wide) group of intellectuals.

Moreover, there was another way of linking liberalism to nationalism. At first sight, Pim Fortuyn's list in the Dutch elections of 2002 was typical of the modern far right. It opposed immigration, on which it blamed 'Islamization of the Netherlands', and wanted to repeal antiracist laws. Yet Fortuyn, who was openly homosexual, denounced Islam as a 'backward religion' that threatened Western toleration and rights for women and gays. Fortuyn was murdered before the elections; his list did well, but succumbed subsequently to in-fighting. By 2010, most supporters had gravitated to the Dutch Party for Freedom, led by Geert Wilders. The latter is closer to the far right elsewhere in Europe, but it too depicts Islam as a threat to freedom, while denouncing Jean-Marie Le Pen as a 'fascist'. This 'liberal intolerance' is more developed in the Netherlands than elsewhere. Nevertheless in France, Marine Le Pen has not wholeheartedly endorsed opposition to gay marriage, and in Switzerland, the xenophobic Democratic Union of the Centre has a gay section.

The re-working of liberalism favoured the far right in a third, contradictory, way. In the 1980s, neo-conservatives, notably Margaret Thatcher in Britain and Ronald Reagan in the USA, began a drive against the left. In economics, that meant the revival of liberal economics, in the form of deregulation. Insofar as it also meant global free trade, neo-conservatism was at odds with the economic nationalism of the New Right, but neo-conservatives justified liberalization as strengthening the nation in the age of global competition. In cultural matters, neo-conservatism was distinctly illiberal, especially regarding immigration and homosexuality.

Thatcher and Reagan were democratic conservatives, but in France, neo-liberalism developed on the far right, for the mainstream resisted it. Moreover, the circumstances in which the FN broke into mass politics recalled the conditions in which fascism had flourished in interwar Europe, in that it appealed largely to disillusioned conservatives. In 1981, in the midst of a global economic crisis, the French Socialists had captured the presidency and for the first time ever formed a government based unequivocally on a left-wing majority. The right, meanwhile, descended into quarrelsome factions, just as neo-conservatism seemed dynamic in other countries. Initially, the FN electorate was relatively bourgeois, elderly, Catholic, conservative, and antisocialist, and the Party programme coincided with this electorate's demands for the free market. The FN's racism reinforced liberal economics, for the Arab was a symbol of the 'unfit', unable to compete in the market, who vegetated on welfare benefits.

Subsequently, the FN moved away from liberal economics, while the mainstream right (inconsistently) embraced it. The FN continues to take most of its voters from the right, particularly from small towns in provincial France. On the local level the FN collaborates politically with the right, not the left. Yet it also became a party of the young, working-class male, who was often unemployed, relatively uneducated, and living in the industrial suburbs of large cities. In the presidential elections of 1995, 30 per cent of workers voted for the FN, more than for the socialists or the communists. There have been tensions within the FN between those who seek alliance with the parliamentary right and those who prefer to target the voters of the left. But by the 2000s, it had largely abandoned neo-conservatism in favour of defending French jobs against globalization and foreign workers—a policy that nevertheless also appeals to a large part of the right. The FN's appeal to the poor has parallels elsewhere in Europe.

Decades of unemployment amongst unskilled young men, thanks to the de-industrialization of Western economies, is an obvious reason for this phenomenon. Russia and the former East Germany also witnessed the collapse of heavy industry and agriculture under the impact of free market reforms, and these sectors provided support for the extreme right. Economic difficulty coincides with a sense of cultural disadvantage. Work no longer provides identity and status for many young men. Given cultural pressure to consume conspicuously, and the linkage of consumer goods to sex appeal, poor young men feel left out. They resent governments that are more inclined to tackle discrimination on grounds of gender, race, or sexual orientation than they are to deal with class inequality—doubtless governments ignore class inequality because it alone is intrinsic to capitalism. Consequently, the far right resents the wealthy and dislikes career women. In ghettoized suburban estates, young white men confront immigrants, whom they blame for crime and attacks on 'their' women, and some are open to parties that cast them as oppressed 'minorities', which in a sense they are. Of course, poor whites are underprivileged members of the *dominant* ethnic group, and consequently they command more sympathy from the police and press than immigrants do, but they hardly count as privileged.

The availability of workers to the far right may owe something to the fact that from the 1990s many socialist parties embraced the neo-conservative agenda. The differences between left and right are attenuated, and both speak largely for those who have gained from the transformation of the economy, leaving the losers without representation. As the left has shifted rightwards in search of electoral success, conservative parties use xenophobia to differentiate themselves from the left. Not to be outdone, the left reassures the electorate that it is not soft on immigrants either. Anti-immigrant policies become respectable, although this respectability is as likely to legitimate the far right as to render it unnecessary. Immigrants are the losers, either way.

It will be obvious from the above that the conditions that produced the modern far right are very different from those from which Fascism and Nazism arose. Nevertheless, even in the interwar years, contexts varied greatly from one part of Europe to another, and indeed even within individual countries people embraced fascism for different reasons.

Conclusion

These case studies show that those who candidly assumed the legacy of fascism rarely enter mainstream politics. Those who have sought to render the extreme right acceptable in an age assumed to be democratic have moved in different directions. Fini's AN was eventually incorporated into the conservative mainstream—albeit the markedly more right-wing mainstream of Berlusconi. At the other extreme, Germany's violent far-right parties, with their large skinhead memberships and history of anti-immigrant violence, have struggled to make an impact.

The most successful of fascism's heirs, like the FN, have transformed themselves into racist and populist parties operating within democratic legality. With some variations, this applies to Jörg Haider's Freedom Party (FPÖ), which won second place in the Austrian general election of October 1999. The FPÖ subsequently survived the death of its leader, EU sanctions, schisms and internal controversies concerning free-market and welfare policies, and is a significant presence in Austrian politics. In Britain, the BNP looked briefly like it might break into the political system, but by 2011 it was suffering from the rise of the UK Independence Party (UKIP), which combined hostility to Eastern European migrants with more traditional conservative antipathies.

There are genuine continuities between interwar fascism and the modern extreme right (extreme nationalism and discrimination against ethnic minorities, antifeminism, antisocialism, populism, hostility to established social and political elites, anticapitalism, and antiparliamentarianism). There are equally significant differences (lack of mass mobilization, paramilitary violence, and the ambition to create a one-party state). More often, the modern far right seeks to exploit the discriminatory potential of democracy rather than overthrow it. This is not to say that the modern far right is 'less evil', or 'less dangerous', than fascism. That's a moral question to which I shall return in the final chapter.

Chapter 7
Fascism, nation, and race

Fascism and Nazism were both racist, and yet Fascism was not racist in the same way that Nazism was. In Nazi Germany, biological racism permeated all aspects of domestic and foreign policy. In Italy, concern with the health of the race was integral to social policy, imperial policy was frankly racist, the regime introduced antisemitic laws, and the Salò Republic colluded in the Final Solution. Yet nobody would pretend that left to their own devices Fascists would have implemented their own Final Solution. So unprecedented is the Nazi crime against the Jews that many scholars have doubted whether Nazism and Fascism can be grouped together as 'fascist'.

Clearly, if we are to use the concept of fascism, then we must remember that it cannot explain the actual histories of any movement or regime, for in that respect differences mattered enormously. Furthermore, we shall see that differences in the race policies of the two regimes, real and imagined, were vitally important in relations between them and in the international reception of fascism.

The race question is equally complex in the recent resurgence of the far right. Anti-immigration policies are universally important but exterminationism is rare. The modern far right apparently rejects the idea of racial inequality—something that was an article of faith for both Fascists and Nazis. Like the South African Apartheid regime, they insist that races (like genders) are 'equal but different'. Cursory examination reveals that the claim is phoney, but it is important nonetheless.

Biological and cultural racism

Before going further, we must make some distinctions, not for the sake of categorization, but because protagonists made them and they had practical consequences, often for who lived and died. First, racism and antisemitism need not go together, for the idea that Jews are a race, not a religion, is relatively recent. Second, we must distinguish different kinds of racism.

Antiracists argue that religious, linguistic, and cultural differences are perfectly acceptable so long as they don't harm anyone. There should be no 'loyalty tests', such as knowledge of the nation's history or support for the national football team. No one is regarded as more likely to have committed a crime because of their ethnic origins, and people who break the law are treated alike. All have the same entitlement to 'due process', and the guilty receive the same punishments—non-citizens do not receive the 'double punishment' of sentence plus deportation, because that would be discriminatory. Antiracists may also advocate *multiculturalism* according to which cultural difference is acceptable as long as it does not harm others.

The most inflexible racism holds that race is determined *biologically*. Biology cannot be changed, and so adopting another nationality is impossible. Indeed, the Nazis believed that assimilated Jews were more dangerous, for they were effectively disguised as Germans. Biological racism may also divide peoples into higher and lower, the latter not clearly distinct from higher animals. These 'sub-humans' might be used in the interests of the higher races, or even killed. Since the late 19th century, elements of the far right had begun to consider that Jews were a race, rather than a religion, and the Nazis took up that idea.

In the early 20th century, most educated Europeans who thought in terms of race were *assimilationists*. They believed that one could be 'assimilated' into the national culture by living in it, learning its values and language, and perhaps practising its religion. Sometimes assimilation was associated with progressive politics, for it implied that anyone could join a nationality. On these grounds, in the 19th century, liberal France and Hungary granted civil rights to Jews—so long as they refrained from public displays of difference. Likewise, in Soviet Russia, Jews climbed to the top of the governmental tree, yet the regime ruthlessly stamped out visible expressions of difference. Suspicion of those who did not conform to the supposed cultural characteristics of the majority often made assimilationism racist, but 'only' the (allegedly) unassimilated would be the targets, not the whole ethnic group. In practice, assimilationist and biological ideas of race were not always distinct, but in some circumstances they had important implications.

Assimilationism in interwar Europe sometimes involved oppressive measures such as the closure of minority language schools. Much depended too on the amount of time said to be required before an individual was assimilated. Barrès had maintained that people imbibed Frenchness through *centuries* of contact with the national soil. He held, moreover, that Jews were urban creatures who could never be fully French because they had never tilled the land. In the interwar years, this 'blood and soil' nationalism was widely prevalent on the European right, fascist and non-fascist, and since it left little scope for ethnic minorities to change their national belonging, it was potentially very exclusionary.

Differences between types of racism were blurred further by the fact that even the Nazis mixed biological and assimilationist reasoning. They forced assimilation of populations they regarded as racially close to Germans. The National Socialist People's

Welfare Organization (NSV) forcibly resettled in Germany Dutch and Norwegian mothers of children born of German fathers. The NSV kidnapped children from Polish orphanages and endeavoured to Germanize them through discipline and hard labour. Nazi 'experts' debated the assimilability of particular populations in learned journals—thereby giving an air of scientific respectability to their policies.

Another complication is that the extreme right has never monopolized racism. Sometimes explicitly, sometimes unconsciously, it has often shaped left-wing thought and practice too. The history of left-wing racism lies outside the scope of this book, but it is worth remembering that the left has usually been more optimistic about the possibility of assimilation, and it has rarely believed that racial policy was a panacea for society's ills. Socialists usually believe class to be more important than race, while liberals emphasize the rights of all people, regardless of origin.

Nazism

Nazi racism might seem straightforward, were it not that at one time certain academic interpretations diminished its significance. Marxists tended to view antisemitism as a means for capitalists to hide the real causes of workers' misery. Weberians argued that the Jew was a convenient symbol of the modern world that fascists disliked so much. These interpretations are valid in themselves, but racism was more than a device to achieve other ends.

Recent interpretations of Nazism have demonstrated that race pervaded all aspects of Nazism. That is not to say that other priorities did not count, or that racism was a 'core' from which everything else stemmed. We shall see that other, sometimes conflicting, priorities were folded into racism (such as the need to avoid offending allies). Even those whom we might regard as at the centre of the regime disagreed on aspects of race policy.

Yet Hitler *believed* that race was the primary force in the world, and that had terrible consequences. He adhered to all the premises of biological racism. In *Mein Kampf*, he sorted races into a hierarchy with Aryans at the summit, assumed that there was a Darwinian struggle for domination between races, and that there was a will to purity within each race. Individuals and groups gained fulfilment through self-sacrifice for the good of the race. For Hitler, the Jews were engaged in a permanent struggle to undermine the Aryan race, especially by promoting cosmopolitan capitalism and communism, and by encouraging war between 'healthy' nations. Hitler also saw prostitution as a way for Jews to corrupt Aryans by transmitting syphilis and hereditary diseases. Hence the Nazis' advocacy of eugenicist solutions to the racial question: selective breeding, sterilization of the unfit, and welfare legislation for the sound elements of the population. Hitler did not speak explicitly of extermination, but the language he used to describe Jews—bacilli, leeches, parasites—legitimated mass murder.

Historians have rightly remarked that during the Nazis' rise to power, as part of their bid for conservative support, the Jews were only one of several enemies attacked by the Nazis (alongside Poles, Catholics, Communists, and Socialists). And since the Jews posed no direct threat, they were not yet the primary target. Yet antisemitism was an obsession with Hitler and his henchmen, and it was implicit in Nazi propaganda all along. Take the poster from the 1932 presidential elections reproduced in Figure 7. The top part depicts a variety of Socialists and Communists under the caption, in pseudo-Hebraic lettering, 'We are voting for Hindenburg!' The pictures beneath, under a heading in traditional Germanic script, are of leading Nazis who will be voting for Hitler. Other posters portray demonic Communists with devilish Jews whispering in their ears.

Although the extermination of the Jews was not inevitable, the great credit earned by the Nazis as victors over the communists and

7. 'We're voting for Hitler'. Poster from the 1932 presidential election campaign

as architect of Germany's national resurrection permitted them to implement their racist designs. Among the first measures taken under the Enabling Act was restriction of Jewish employment in the civil service and professions. In 1935, Jews were forbidden to marry or to have sexual relations with Aryans. Aside from explicitly racial laws, other legislation had racial objectives. The Law for the Prevention of Hereditarily Diseased Progeny (July 1933) permitted compulsory sterilization of certain categories of the population. Incentives to women to devote themselves to home and family were intended to increase the quantity of the racially desirable population. In 1935, a certificate of racial fitness was required of all those who wished to marry. Marriage loans and rewards for large families were refused to 'those of lesser racial value'. Shortly before the war, there began a programme of killing the psychiatrically ill and mentally handicapped. All these measures were intended to create a racially pure, physically and mentally healthy population, fit to make war on inferior races and conquer *lebensraum* in the east. Initially, the hope was that life would become so uncomfortable for Jews that they would emigrate, but the government's reluctance to let them take assets with them, and of foreign governments to accept Jews, thwarted these hopes. The pogrom of 9–10 November 1938—*Kristallnacht*—resulted from pressure by Nazi activists coupled with Goebbels' yearning for favour with Hitler. It was followed by state plunder of Jewish wealth. Emigration remained the goal, but ominously the SS gained greater power over antisemitic policy.

The final radicalization of Nazi policy towards the Jews was precipitated by war in the East. It must be remembered, though, that war against 'Judeo-Bolshevism' had long been the Nazis' goal. In January 1939, Hitler declared that should Jewish finance succeed in plunging Europe into war, the result wouldn't be 'Bolshevizing of the earth, and thus a victory of Jewry, but the annihilation of the Jewish race in Europe'. Some Nazis still interpreted such outbursts as a legitimation of 'voluntary' emigration; others thought it meant forced emigration to Madagascar or Poland—policies which, it was accepted, would entail many fatalities. Hitler's proclamations also licensed the killing of Jews in occupied Poland. From December 1939, ghettoization, forced labour, and expulsion represented a

8. A Nazi *Einsatzgruppe* murders Jews at Sniatyn, Poland (now in the Ukraine), 11 May 1943

significant move away from the rules normally governing human behaviour. Then, in preparation for the invasion of Russia, instructions were issued to SS special squads—the *Einsatzgruppen*—to kill Communist officials above an undefined rank, Jews in party and state employment, radicals, saboteurs, propagandists, and others. These orders gave an enormous degree of latitude to the *Einsatzgruppen*, all the more so as it was difficult in practice to establish who was a Jew or a Communist. The *Einsatzgruppen* murdered hundreds of thousands of Jews in local 'actions' (see Figure 8). By the end of the year, as Hitler and his subordinates predicted fulfilment of the prophecy of January 1939, the question was not whether, but where, how, and when the Jews would be killed. In early 1942, it was decided that Jews were either to be worked to death in camps or killed immediately. In total, around six million Jews perished.

Crucially, though, until spring 1942, leading Nazis assumed that the *final* solution would come after the expected victory over Bolshevism. Only when they realized that the war would be long

115

did they decide to implement it during the war itself. This murderous shift had consequences for Nazi relations with their foreign allies, for the murder of the Jews had been part of a plan for a wider racial remaking of Europe. The Nazis knew that frontier adjustments and resettlements would divide their allies, whom they needed more than ever in a long war. Consequently, they could only focus on the Jews. Since the 1930s, antisemitism had been one of the main ways in which the Nazis had spread their influence at the expense of Fascism, and now they sought to strengthen their alliances by involving their allies in the Final Solution, which became a test of loyalty. Their allies knew that, and as the fortunes of war turned against the Axis, they began to differentiate their own racism from that of the Nazis. Distinctions between kinds of racism became immensely important—which had major implications for Germany's number one ally.

Italian Fascism, antisemitism, and race

Historians used to hold that Fascist antisemitism was imported from Germany. They rightly stressed that antisemitism was weaker in Italy, and that there were Jews in prominent positions in the Fascist Party and regime. One of Mussolini's mistresses, Margherita Sarfatti, was Jewish.

Recent research has shown that there was nevertheless a tradition of racism and antisemitism in Italy. Since its foundation in 1910, the Italian Nationalist Association had used racism to justify imperialism, and claimed that eugenics could improve the Italian race. Before the 1930s, the major practical consequence of racism was domestic. Fascism sought to complete Italian Unification, an objective justified by the need to compete with 'brown and yellow races'. Nationalists looked to the eugenicist academics, such as the anthropologist Guiseppe Sergi, who claimed that improving the quality and quantity of the population would allow the Italian people to realize its destiny of imperial conquest.

Completing unification entailed hostility to minorities, who seemed especially dangerous where borders were disputed. During the rise to power, the *squadristi* attacked 'inferior' Slavic minorities in the northwest. In power, the regime forcibly assimilated the German minority of the South Tyrol, which had been annexed by Italy after the Great War. The regime cited dubious anthropological and historical evidence supposedly proving that Tyrolean German-speakers were really Italians who had been Germanized under the Habsburg Empire. These speculations legitimated the Italianization of surnames, suppression of German newspapers, compulsory use of Italian in the administration, and closure of German schools. Hitler turned a blind eye to this discrimination, for he wanted Italian friendship.

Antisemitism was less widespread, but it existed. The INA was not officially antisemitic, but it sometimes accused Jews of lacking patriotism. The major source of antisemitism was the Catholic press, which since the 1890s, had treated Jews not only as the enemy of Christianity, but a race, and advocated discrimination and even expulsion. Fascism drew on both Catholics and Nationalists, and so imported antisemitism. It was especially marked in the circles around Roberto Farinacci, which opposed 'normalization' of Fascism and wanted a more thoroughgoing revolution. These radicals also criticized Germany, so it follows that their views were independent of admiration of Nazism.

Notwithstanding, before the 1930s, race and still less antisemitism did not inform domestic or foreign policy as pervasively as it would in Germany, and Fascists were more interested in raising the birthrate than in eliminating the unfit. Indeed, in his bid for influence in movements outside Italy, Mussolini promoted Fascist universalism as an alternative to Nazi racism. In 1930, he ridiculed biological racism. He regarded race as a 'feeling', which, by implication anyone could acquire.

From the mid-1930s, the racism and antisemitism of the regime intensified. From 1934–5 Fascists invoked 'African inferiority' to justify the invasion of Ethiopia (an action that Germany alone among the powers supported). Colonialism implied greater attention to the integrity of the Italian race itself. Given that many regarded Jews as part of the Italian race, antisemitism did not necessarily follow. But by the mid-1930s so many foreign fascist movements had turned to Nazism that Mussolini felt that the only way to compete was to strengthen his own antisemitic followers. Moreover, an indirect consequence of the rise of Nazism was that Mussolini became convinced that Jews were the primary force behind antifascism.

The regime officially adopted biological racism and antisemitism. From 1938 Jews were removed from the professions and their businesses were confiscated. Some Fascists mocked the new turn, but none resigned. Perhaps the fact the regime's spokesmen still sometimes used cultural and/or religious definitions of race comforted them. From 1939, a provision permitting Jews to prove that they had a biologically 'Aryan' parent introduced much scope for arbitrariness and corruption.

From 1942, the distinction between cultural and biological racism mattered once again, for as the Allies approached Italy the alliance with Germany looked unwise. When the Germans demanded deportation of Jews, the Italian government responded that it must protect those with Italian citizenship—Italian occupation authorities in France, Greece, and Croatia refused to hand over Jews. The Germans admitted that Italian uncooperativeness had encouraged other allies to resist.

After Italy capitulated in 1943, the Salò Republic took control of the north, and gave the Germans greater leverage. The dependence of Salò on German money and troops does not entirely absolve Fascists of responsibility. Even there, the Germans found that they could not deport Jews without Italian help, and so they exploited the Salò government's independent decision to intern all Jews, and used the Italian police. Nevertheless, over 80 per cent of Jews escaped thanks to the solidarity of the population.

Racism in occupied Europe

The Germans recognized that disputes about the meaning of racism and its policy implications mattered in occupied Europe. As German victories became rare and at Stalingrad in January 1943 turned to defeat, the Nazis intensified persecution of the Jews. Now, allied regimes, whether fascist or conservative, were more reluctant to be compromised by assisting deportations, and distinctions between assimilationism and biological antisemitism once more became politically important.

In Romania, the Iron Guard saw religion as the basis of the nation, and sometimes it condemned biological racism. Yet it used racism to discredit the pro-French liberal elite. It depicted itself as the emanation of the Dacian peasantry—the supposedly original inhabitants of Romania before the Roman conquest. The Iron Guard claimed that the present-day Romanian governing elite issued from the Roman or Turko-Greek occupying powers, and had corrupted the country by favouring Jewish and French influences. By the late 1930s, expressions of exterminationist antisemitism were common in Romania, and the outbreak of war, under the authoritarian Antonescu government, there were many pogroms and massacres—including a particularly murderous one in Iaşi, where Codreanu had murdered the police chief. Romania contributed forces to the invasion of Russia, which joined with German forces in massacring Jews. The Romanian government initially assented to Germany's deportation plans, but by the end of 1942 they were refusing to hand Jews over, partly because protests from the Church and royal family ensured that the religious definiton of the nation once more became important.

It is no accident that Italy, Romania, and Bulgaria, which had all resisted deportations, changed sides. Elsewhere, the Nazis could only enforce deportation through direct pressure and the assistance of fascist diehards who had little popular support—as events in Italy showed. The Hungarian regime resisted demands to deport its Jewish population until the country was occupied in 1944. In France too, the government developed doubts. In late 1942, it resisted denaturalizing French Jews, but since it had willingly assisted the deportation of French and foreign Jews, it was locked into the German sphere. Once the whole country was occupied, in November 1942, the Germans used fascist minorities to help them deport foreign and French Jews alike, but as in Italy the help of the population saved many others.

The contemporary far right and racism

In pursuit of respectability, the contemporary far right denies that it is racist. Like the New Right, it claims that the real racists are the architects of globalization and multiculturalism, who undermine national differences.

David Duke, a former KKK member, set up the National Association for the Advancement of White People to make white nationalism more acceptable to the mainstream. The group maintained that 'there should be equal rights and opportunities for all, including Whites'.

Likewise, in 2002, The British National Party (BNP) maintained that it was not racist because

> 'Racism' is when you 'hate' another ethnic group. We don't 'hate' black people, we don't 'hate' Asians, we don't oppose any ethnic group for what God made them, they have a right to their own identity as much as we do, all we want to do is to preserve the ethnic and cultural identity of the British people. We want the same human rights as everyone else...

> (www.bnp.org.uk/faq.html, 2002)

It is easy to expose the racist assumptions of such assertions, for each race must remain pure, and that legitimates discrimination against minorities. It is races that have equal rights, not individual people. Notwithstanding, racism remains complex, and is entangled with other priorities. Take the BNP again. In 2002, as it was embarking on its a ballot-box campaign, it defined the nation racially:

> the native peoples who have lived in these islands since before the Stone Age, and the relatively small numbers of peoples of almost identical stock, such as the Saxons, Vikings and Normans, and the Irish, who have come here and assimilated.

Admission of the possibility of assimilation should not be dismissed. In 2013, a BNP journalist claimed that although white immigration presented problems for jobs and housing, at least their children's children might become British. It was preferable, though, that nationalists should have more babies, a 'fun' way of rebuilding 'the ethnic British race'. In fact, once the BNP turns to non-whites, biological assumptions predominate. It opposed mixed marriages, because 'all species and races of life on this planet are beautiful and must be preserved'.

For the BNP the duty of the government is to foster the 'uniqueness' of the people. Consequently, it advocates severe restrictions upon immigration, and calls for voluntary repatriation (although its leader, Nick Griffin, admits that he would prefer all non-whites to leave). Preference in the job market would be given to 'natives', while business would be restored to 'native' ownership. Perhaps it expects that ethnic minorities would find life so difficult that they would leave. The French FN certainly hopes that immigrants will quit the towns it governs, but in principle it prefers compulsion. Jorg Haider in Austria claimed to have 'nothing against those who've been here for 20–30 years and have made a living', only that he wants to turn new arrivals away.

Often, antipathy to Muslims cross-cuts racism—for Pim Fortuyn, the late Dutch far-right leader, religion counted more than race. In September 2001, following the destruction of the World Trade Center in New York by terrorist suicide pilots, mainstream Western politicians (with the exception of Berlusconi) carefully distinguished between majority Muslim opinion and a minority of zealots. The BNP agreed that not all Muslims were fanatics (liberal language again), but saw Islam itself as dangerous. Just as Hitler believed the Jews were engaged in a campaign to 'Jewify' Germany, so the BNP believed that through 'indoctrination' in schools, high birth rates, and immigration, fundamentalists aimed to turn Britain into an Islamic republic. Not all neo-fascists share this hatred of Islam. Some German neo-Nazis, perhaps remembering Nazi overtures to Islam, welcomed 11 September as an attack on their common enemy—America.

It is uncertain how far-right policies would play out in practice. One uncertainty is how second or third generation offspring of 'immigrants' would be treated. Would they face discrimination in the job market and welfare system? One could expect conflicts between hard-liners and moderates within the far right. It is certain that life would not be easy for those considered ethnically alien, all the more so as racial purity is an impossible dream. Should the white population of Australia be repatriated to Europe? Must the million retired British people in the Mediterranean lands return?

The lesson of history is that racial homogenization requires enormous compulsion and a radical break with democratic and humane values. Even the Nazi's gigantic efforts produced mixed results. To exterminate the Jews, they had to mobilize huge resources and negate everything hitherto considered decent. Even then, they failed to make Germany racially homogeneous. The war machine's desire for labour dictated the forced immigration of seven million foreign workers and slaves. Although these labourers were subjected to unimaginably harsh treatment, the regime could not prevent loving relations developing between Germans and foreigners. Paranoia about racial mixing drove the regime to greater, but equally futile, excess.

History also shows that the oppressiveness of racism is exacerbated by its arbitrariness. No one has shown that differences between people living on opposite sides of national boundaries, which were usually the result of dynastic accident or the fortunes of war, are related to 'deep psychology' or genetics. Neither has anyone shown that tiny genetic differences of people with different skin colour have any effect on cultures. Moreover, the differences within nations are as great or greater than those between nations. Yet the very vagueness of their principles permits racists to adapt their ideas to whatever purpose they espouse. Earlier in the century, it was customary to evoke the fundamentally different characteristics of Aryans and Latins. Now all Europeans are said to be united in a struggle against Islam. Some see the English and Irish as racially different, others do not. Needless to say, such disagreements are not the product of scientific investigation. Racism is a prejudice erected into a system.

Chapter 8
Fascism, women, and gender

Conceiving fascism as a form of totalitarianism or as a political religion has the disadvantage of positing a simple dichotomy between the active elite and a mass that is manipulated and undifferentiated, united in idolizing the leader. The concept of governmentality may also exaggerate the coherence of fascist ideology and of modern techniques of rule—the public health, welfare, and other programmes that were intended to secure the health of the nation and race.

Certainly fascists often evoked the 'mass' or the 'herd'. However, they did not imagine this mass as homogeneous, but as a hierarchy in which each group contributed in its own way to the good of the nation under the leadership of an elite, just as in the body the head directs the lower organs. Fascists also promised to overcome class and gender conflict, to unite the community, but it never occurred to them that classes or genders would cease to exist. One of fascists' grievances against socialists, feminists, and Jews was precisely that they undermined supposedly natural differences, and doubtless many people embraced fascism because they thought that it would restore them—after all, Hitler had a very traditional view of the roles of men and women. However, fascists also sought to address 'legitimate grievances' and thus to tackle problems that caused workers and women to turn to socialism and feminism.

The results were complex. On the one hand, the theatre of mass rallies and ambitious new leisure programmes blurred or disguised social distinctions. On the other hand, the party created groups exclusively for workers, women, and others which perpetuated existing social and gender differences. The purpose of these groups was to allow workers and women to defend their separate interests, but in such a way that they would not harm the general interest (hence the need to destroy socialist and feminist groups). Fascist unions and women's groups, coupled with ambitious social policies, would win workers and women back into the national community. This aspiration meant engaging with a well-established body of ideas and policies concerning health, welfare, and the workplace that were the subject of great debate, and which socialists and feminists had helped to develop. Moreover, these organizations provided opportunities for political action on the part of workers and women. In this chapter, I shall chart the fortunes of women in fascism before turning to workers in the next.

At first sight, Fascism is quintessentially male. It evokes the uniformed street-fighter of the interwar years and the skinhead of modern times. Fascism dislikes feminism as much as it does socialism, and sees women's primary function as domestic and reproductive, while the modern far right claims that the sexes—like races—are 'equal but different'. Fascists nearly always categorize themselves as 'not feminist', but their attempts to refute feminism drag them into implicit dialogue with it in spite of themselves. Consequently, relations between the sexes represent yet another source of disagreement among fascists.

Many Europeans were convinced that the Great War had unbalanced relations between the sexes. Women had taken male jobs, and were suspected of living independent and frivolous lives whilst men endured the trenches. Even more worryingly, the involvement of women in the war effort stimulated the development of women's organizations, some of them feminist.

Afterwards women gained the vote in many countries. Bourgeois women adopted simpler forms of dress, more suited to working life, a fashion seen by some as de-feminizing them. Pierre Drieu La Rochelle, French veteran, novelist, and future fascist lamented, 'this civilization no longer has sexes', and saw that as a sign of general social decay. He was not alone in seeing 'feminine' passions in the rebellions of workers and national minorities. These fears converged in the campaign, common to most European countries, to compensate for war deaths by raising the birthrate. 'Natalist' campaigns implied that women were primarily mothers, and should perhaps be forbidden other roles.

Fascists saw male veterans as the virile agents of national regeneration. Service in the trenches proved their devotion to the nation, and promoted bravery, heroism, self-sacrifice, comradeship, the ability to endure suffering, and obedience—qualities that should be transferred to society as a whole. Codreanu called for 'a new type of hero in the warring sense, a social hero, a hero of work'. His model was the medieval king Stephen the Great, celebrated for his military prowess and fathering of children. These ideals were taken furthest in the SS, which represented a male martial order inspired by the Japanese Samurai, Teutonic Knights, and Jesuits. Fascists did not value masculinity per se—only that of the dominant race. The rest were 'feminine races'. Some Nazis saw Italians in the same way: as a feminine people operating through plots rather than manly openness.

It is no shock to discover that most fascists hated homosexuals. Some scholars consider that homophobia derived from repressed homosexuality. As evidence, they point to the homoerotic dress and lifestyle of the SS, or to the contemporary German neo-Nazi who argues that homosexuality strengthens the bonds between real men. Take also the example of Ernst Röhm, leader of the Nazi SA. In many ways, Röhm was typical of fascists; his facial scars reminded his comrades of his war service and courage. He expected women to remain silent, and saw the Weimar Republic as an unmanly regime characterized by feminine parliamentary chattering, in which femininized Jews and Communists were too influential. In fact, Röhm's homosexuality was widely known. He avoided accusations of unmanliness through intensely male display.

Actually, there is no reason to believe that homosexuals are overrepresented among fascists. The truth is probably more prosaic. Fascists were particularly hostile to homosexuals because they *feared* that their all-male communities would expose them to accusations of homosexuality. That does not prevent the use of accusations of homosexuality, true and false, as a weapon in struggles within fascist and indeed modern far-right parties.

That Röhm rose to the top of the Nazi hierarchy highlights fascism's ability to attract radicals of diverse shades. Röhm was radical in the sense that he criticized 'bourgeois morality', and hoped that Nazism would have done with bourgeois hypocrisy and usher in a new manly order. Those who interpreted the Nazi revolution in this way were a small minority, and they stood little chance of turning their dreams into reality. Indeed, Röhm's 'perversion' was a pretext for the suppression of the SA in June 1934. Thereafter, the Nazis increased their persecution of homosexuals, many of whom died in concentration camps or were 'treated' for their 'illness'.

As for women, fascists wavered between contempt and idealization of them as mothers. The Italian Futurist Filippo Marinetti was famous for his 'scorn for women'. Some Nazis campaigned against women's right to wear make-up or smoke in public. The Romanian Iron Guard newspaper declared in 1937 that 'today's "intellectual" woman is an element utterly sterile for society'. Fascist regimes attempted to remove women from the labour market and restrict their access to education. Whether in Germany, Italy, or Croatia, fascists assigned to women the task of producing the future citizens, soldiers, and mothers of the race. Women must inculcate national values in their children, and as consumers (rather than producers) they must ensure that families consumed national products.

There was a contradiction in these policies. Although fascists wanted women to remain in the home, they politicized functions once regarded simply as 'domestic': reproduction, education, and consumption all became national duties. Furthermore, to teach women their domestic duties, fascists encouraged them to join organizations linked to the party—to return women to the home, fascism took them out of the home. At a time when most conservative organizations had few female members, fascist organizations possessed significant women's sections.

In Italy, there were some 2,000 female Fascists in 1921. Women's membership stagnated in the later 1920s, but rocketed in the 1930s, as the regime 'went to the masses'. At the time of the seizure of power, about 8 per cent of Nazi Party members were women. In 1931, women's sections had been amalgamated into the National Socialist Frauenschaft (NSF), which, after the seizure of power, took control of all remaining women's groups and recruited over two million members by 1938. Both Nazis and Fascists held that women could only be incorporated into the nation if their special needs and interests as women were recognized. So they made women's organizations part of the party or regime—just as they attempted to incorporate the labour movement. Fascism, in consequence, attracted women with diverse agendas (see Figure 9). While fascists hardly qualified as 'feminist', given that they endeavoured to eliminate rival groups (with greater success in Germany than in Italy), they did attract women with diverse agendas, including some feminists.

That fascism should have done so is less surprising if one is aware of the diversity of feminism. Some feminists—often known as familial feminists—were less interested in the vote than in protecting women as women—they demanded protection against male alcoholism, suppression of prostitution, and improvement in

9. Female members of the British Union of Fascists salute Sir Oswald Mosley, 1936

women's rights at work. If such feminists were prepared to abandon representative democracy (a big if), they potentially had something in common with fascists, for both in their own rather different ways saw women as equal but different.

Fascism also attracted *anti*feminist women who agreed with fascist men that women's place was in the home. For many bourgeois women, after all, the family offered privileges—control over children and servants within an extended household. As 'carers' women could be involved in important charitable organizations, sometimes with influence on government policy. Such women attacked feminism—along with socialism, liberalism, and democracy—for undermining charity, the family, and the supply of domestic servants. Despite their conservatism, these women didn't always feel that conventional conservative organizations paid sufficient attention to the family. In Germany, poor rural women may have voted for the Nazis because they saw feminism as a bourgeois fashion accessory.

In Italy, many women's organizations saw the old Liberal regime as unresponsive to their concerns, and so favoured the nationalist opposition, including the Fascists, whose 1919 programme included women's suffrage. Under fascism they championed a 'Latin feminism', which subordinated individual rights to tradition, family, and race, and which was antisocialist and antiliberal. In Germany Emma Hadlich claimed that before foreign influence had corrupted it German society was based on equality of the sexes. In Britain, women won the vote in 1918 and 1928, but some feminists were disappointed that this victory did not bring real political influence, and they hoped that fascism might remedy that.

Fascism, then, won support from a range of women's groups, feminist and non-feminist, formerly liberal, conservative, and socialist. The engagement of women in fascist movements and regimes illuminates again the struggle to define fascism. The most radical of the women did not fare well in fascist regimes, for male activists (who had more power) had become fascists precisely to restore the 'normal' relationship between the sexes. Mussolini soon lost interest in female suffrage and ensured that women's sections were subordinated in principle to male branches. In Germany Hadlich's views were refuted by Alfred Rosenberg, who asserted that ancient German society had been patriarchal. In 1934, Hitler told Nazi women that there was no room for a battle of the sexes within Nazism. Both regimes became more concerned with persuading women to have children—the leader of the NSF, Gertrud Scholtz-Klink, led from the front by bearing eleven. The great majority of women within fascist movements were confined to activities generally considered to be suited to their nature—essentially welfare work.

The defeat of these radicals did not mean that women played a passive role or that fascism became homogenous. Even those

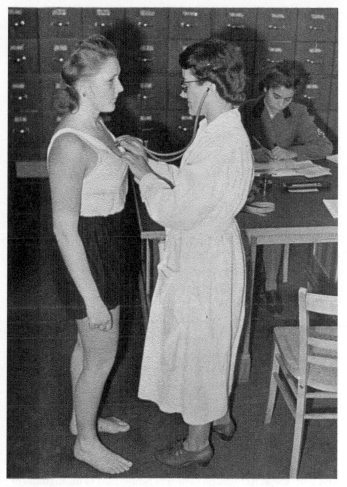

10. A female world? A doctor examines a new recruit to the Reich Community Service Agency, 6 September 1940

engaged in apparently humble tasks such as knitting socks or collecting food for the poor were engaged in activity outside the home, as part of a complex organization directed largely by women (see Figure 10). Further up the hierarchy, the women's sections of fascist movements and regimes employed small armies of health visitors, nurses, domestic science teachers, and social workers. Male fascists might have seen women's work as secondary, but the women concerned did not. They quietly struggled with men to extend their areas of competence and to invest their professions with a status equal to that of doctors and lawyers. For them, welfare was fundamental to the achievement of a harmonious, mobilized nation. Fascist movements demanded, and regimes implemented, welfare provisions, many of which seemed to fulfil long-standing desires of the women's movement (family allowances, marriage loans, improved health care at work, etc.).

These measures weren't primarily intended to increase the choices open to women, but to serve the supposed needs of the party, nation, and race. In Germany, only Aryan women were considered sufficiently 'evolved' to be capable of fulfilling the maternal role or of bearing 'fit' children. Encouraged by Himmler, the SS went as far as to protect unmarried mothers—so long as they and their offspring were racially acceptable. In Italy, 'impeding the fertility of the Italian people' by promoting birth control was designated a crime of state, and the objective of social policy was to improve the race. Also, welfare was distributed according to unofficial political criteria, so that those unfriendly to the regime didn't benefit. In France, the welfare organizations of the Croix de feu and Parti social français on principle refused aid to immigrants or their families, although female activists often ignored the ban.

The contemporary far right and women

The position of women in contemporary far-right parties is not dissimilar. These groups are heavily masculine in style, as demonstrated by Le Pen's belief that French chivalry is the answer to feminism, or by skinheads' football violence. Le Pen allotted to women the 'quasi-divine' mission of transmitting life and 'educating the hearts, minds, and sensibilities of children and adolescents'. The BNP proposes financial incentives for women to have children in order to combat the supposedly dangerous low birth rate and to end discrimination against the family. As in the past, pro-natalism and racism are connected: since labour shortages will no longer be made up through immigration, women must have more babies, and only 'native' women will be encouraged to reproduce.

These policies also reflect the fear, familiar to students of the interwar years, that women are taking over men's jobs. As Le Pen says, interference in the normal allocation of tasks between the genders could lead 'men to take themselves for women, and women taking themselves for men'. These worries are amplified by chronic unemployment amongst the unskilled male working class, and by the conviction of men in employment that 'positive discrimination' in favour of women harms male prospects. Furthermore, as the right worries less about socialism and communism, marriage, divorce, abortion, and sexuality have become more central to politics. In 2012–13, the extension of marriage rights to gay couples in a number of countries reinforced fears that proper gender roles were under threat.

Women, nevertheless, join and vote for far-right parties. Their position is somewhat different to that of women in earlier fascist movements, for although equality remains a long way off, women's position has changed. Thanks to television, cinema, falling religious practice, and the changing nature of education, the range of options visible to women is greater and their *expectations* are higher. And although most women reject the feminist label, they take for granted many of the conquests of feminism. Le Pen's chivalry did not prevent his ex-wife from satirizing his views on the family by appearing as a maid in a pornographic *Playboy* photo-shoot. His daughter, Marine, now leads the party and she is an archetypal working mother.

Far-right movements promise to respect the advances made by women but they attack feminists, and they advocate policies that would actually remove many gains. We cannot say how such tensions would work out in practice, but we can say that implementation of the extreme right's policies towards women would again mean breaking with liberal democracy.

Chapter 9
Fascism and class

At one time, some scholars saw fascism almost exclusively in relation to class. For Marxists, it was a dictatorship of the most reactionary elements of capitalism, or the expression of an alliance of capitalists with the petty bourgeoisie. For Weberians, fascism represented a last-ditch bid by the 'traditional elites' to defend themselves against 'modernization'. We might at this stage add a further theory, also rooted in Weber, which sees fascism as expressing the petty bourgeoisie's hostility to both big capital and organized labour. Marxists and Weberians differ in which class they hold responsible for fascism (and in the way they define class), but both scrutinize the actions, words, and writings of fascists for evidence of the 'underlying interests' of the classes they see as crucial. Marxists detect beneath fascists' nationalism the effort of capitalists to divert workers away from socialism. Similarly, Weberians read antisemitic texts as attempts to demonize the modern world in the person of the Jew or for evidence of the dilemmas of the petty bourgeoisie.

Totalitarian theorists, in contrast, deny the importance of class. Fascists, they say, sought to secure the total loyalty of the people to the national community, above and beyond class allegiances. We saw in the previous chapter that political religions theory also tends to flatten out social differences in an undifferentiated mass, while the concept of governmentality may exaggerate the seamlessness and effectiveness of 'techniques of rule'.

There is some truth in all the above views. Some Fascists quite explicitly declared that they were defending the bourgeoisie, while others claimed that their primary goal was to create a totalitarian community. These two apparently contradictory perspectives are actually compatible. Fascists' mental picture of the ideal community was not an abstract thing, but was made from various preconceptions, so they assumed that the existence of the working-class was a normal part of social relations, and wanted to integrate it *as a class* into the totalitarian community. They would achieve that objective first by eliminating those who corrupted the working class (communists, Jews), thereby ensuring that workers' groups would only make demands that were compatible with community health. Second, fascism would address the material problems that had allowed communism to flourish. Third, attention to workers' conditions would improve the 'quality' of the working class, and ensure that it better served the general interest. The two latter aspirations obliged fascists to draw on a diverse body of social policies and practices pertaining to the proletariat, family, and race that actually crossed political boundaries, and which were marked by many controversies, which, we shall see, continued under fascism. Indeed, in the International Labour Organization (a League of Nations body), Italian Fascist representatives discussed reforms with socialists and trade unionists.

The resulting diversity of fascism was such that potentially any social group could find something to please it. Only by exploring fascism *in context* can we explain who actually supported it and why. I shall look at the question from two angles. I shall examine the social make-up and motivations of fascist supporters, and then ask how the strategies of fascist activists shaped the appeal of fascism.

Activists and voters

There was much variation in support for Fascism and Nazism in class terms. Confining our attention to the much-studied Nazi electorate, we may see that although the Nazis' appeal was skewed towards the bourgeoisie, it also gained considerable support from workers, and was more of an 'all-class' party than were any of its German rivals. French fascism in the interwar years shows a similarly broad appeal combined with over-representation of the middle classes.

There are also intriguing national differences. Whereas in Germany, public-sector teachers and civil servants preferred the Nazis, their counterparts in France were attracted to the left. In Hungary, we find stronger working-class and landless labourer support for fascism than elsewhere. Romanian fascism was mainly backed by peasants and students.

If we take into account other influences on the fascist vote, the picture becomes still more complex. In Germany, Protestant workers in smaller industries were likely to vote Nazi, while Catholic workers voted for the Catholic Centre or the Communists, and Protestant workers in large industries voted for the Socialists. In France, we discover that the Catholic bourgeoisie was more likely to join fascist organizations than was the anticlerical bourgeoisie. We also find that male workers in French heavy industry were less attracted to fascist trade unions than were female workers in the textile industry. Further examples would only confuse. The point is that class was an important influence on vote, but not the only one: gender, geography, and religion mattered too. We may also deduce that the diversity of political attitudes in any given class means that its members must have disagreed on what their interests were, and we may doubt that activists were primarily defined by class at all.

It is also important to remember that activists helped shape fascism's appeal. Too often, activists are seen as expressing underlying social forces—socialist activists are said to 'speak for' working-class interests, while conservative or fascist activists speak for the bourgeoisie. Anyone who knows political activists will realize that they aren't quite like the rest of us. They are convinced that they possess privileged insight into the organization of society and have a mission to persuade everyone else of the validity of their views. The socialist activist, for example, doesn't just articulate the workers' feelings—s/he tries to *persuade* workers that her or his interest lies in embracing one form of socialism, not that of a rival socialist school, political Catholicism, or even fascism. So activists don't just reflect the views of those they seek to represent—they try to shape the way in which people see their interests. We must take seriously those who formulated party propaganda and decided to whom it should be addressed.

Take Nazism. The party's decision to shift its propaganda towards the bourgeoisie after 1930 was a decisive moment in its history. It made a breakthrough with the votes of farmers, the petty bourgeoisie and bourgeoisie. Yet activists also continued to target propaganda widely by emphasizing the nation, and to express popular opposition to an allegedly corrupt and foreign political establishment—potentially a very broad appeal indeed. In contrast, the Socialists appealed especially to the male working class, communists to the male unemployed, and the Catholic Centre to the Catholic minority. Nazi activists endeavoured to channel the resentment of small shopkeepers against 'Jewish' department store owners. They won the support of workers by incorporating the symbols of the left into a nationalist and antisemitic programme: red flags modified with swastikas, or the grinning, gluttonous, top-hatted, cigar-smoking capitalist. Nazis told workers that their enemy was not business, but Jewish business. This nationalist anticapitalism had the advantage of being relatively attractive to many employers, for it spared German capitalists the blame for the workers' plight.

The Nazis were most successful in becoming what many parties have attempted to be—a national party that amalgamated otherwise antagonistic groups into a single movement. However, the success of this strategy was not automatic. Nationalism does not have an inherently broader appeal than class—it all depends how the terms are defined. Indeed, the Nazi conception of the nation was also influenced by 'biases' that potentially restricted its appeal. Many Nazis saw Germany as intrinsically Protestant or even pagan, a view that excluded Catholic workers from their electorate.

The appeal of fascism in class terms is best understood as the product of an exchange between the strategies of fascist activists (with their unacknowledged biases) and the aspirations of particular groups (with their unacknowledged biases). The resulting variability doesn't mean that fascism's class composition is unimportant. On the contrary, it mattered very much, because the different groups that backed fascism differed greatly in the amount of power available to them. I shall illustrate this point through a brief examination of two key terms in the fascist lexicon: 'national socialism' and corporatism.

National socialism

Back in 1898, Maurice Barrès presented the electoral programme of the 'National Socialist Republican Committee' of Nancy:

> Against a policy that aims only to satisfy animosities, and of which the only driving force is the lust for power, I come anew to oppose the *national* and *social* ideas which you have already acclaimed and which you will not today repudiate.
>
> ... In the top ranks of society, in the heart of the provinces, in the moral and material sphere, in commerce, industry, agriculture, even in the shipyards where they compete with French workers, foreigners are poisoning us like parasites.

> One vital principle that should underlie the new French policy is to
> protect all its nationals against this invasion, and to be aware of that
> brand of socialism that is so cosmopolitan, or rather so German,
> that it would weaken the country's defences.

For Barrès, internationalist socialism—Marxism—constituted a
menace to the French nation, indeed to the French race, for it was
a 'German' ideology. He called for a socialism that would be
national in two senses: it would protect those workers with roots
in the national soil and it would reconcile hitherto opposed classes
by ensuring that each subordinated its special interests to the
national good. Capitalists would be nicer to workers, and so the
latter would have no need of socialism.

Barrès called not for the suppression of property but for a change
in the *spirit* of class relations. This formula was less scary for
capitalists than was Marxism. Yet Barrès proposed reforms such
as a graduated income tax and profit sharing, which might seem
tame to contemporary eyes, but were opposed absolutely—even
hysterically—by mainstream conservatives then. Neither were
local steel magnates enthralled by Barrès's desire to stem the flow
of cheap foreign labour. In the event, Barrès's programme did
appeal to some disenchanted conservatives in Nancy, but not to
enough of them to get him elected.

Twenty-seven years later, Hitler, to whom the judge had granted a
degree of latitude unusual for a defendant, addressed the jurors at
his trial for his part on the Beer-Hall putsch:

> The National Socialist movement of what was then the Workers'
> Party adopted as its first principle the realization that the Marxist
> movement was to be fought to the end; second the realization that
> the revolution [of 1918], as the consequence of Marxism and of an
> unprecedented criminal act, was not a matter of the German
> bourgeoisie becoming national once more: the problem is that the
> German working people, the broad masses, must be made

national again. That means not just a pure, I mean passive, relationship to nationalism, but an active fight against those who have ruined it until now. Besides, it is ridiculous to want to nationalize a people at a time when hundreds of thousands are working on all sides to de-nationalize the people, and these hundreds of thousands, who also brought about the revolution, do not even belong to the race. Thus, the Marxist problem has become a racial problem, the most serious and deepest problem of the day.

Hitler might not have shared Barrès's literary gifts, but his assumptions were similar. Internationalist Marxist socialism is the enemy of the German race, and workers could only be reincorporated into the nation if it was eliminated. *National* socialism reconciles the classes also by formation of 'national' bodies that would reconcile workers' demands with national priorities. Potentially, acceptance of workers' legitimate demands set it against capitalists. Indeed, fascists did wish to subordinate business to the collective good, but did not contest the existence of capitalism per se. The outcome of such intentions was hard to predict.

Corporatism

Hitler saw corporatism, sometimes dismissed by contemporary scholars as a smokescreen for the untrammelled power of big business, as a key way to reintegrate the workers into the nation. However, corporatism was not intrinsically fascist, and there were many versions of it circulating in contemporary society. At its simplest, it meant that bodies with a stake in the economy—trade unions, employers' organizations, groups representing families or farmers, and so on—took decisions about social and economic policy, rather than the government or parliament. At one time or another, most postwar Western democracies have practised corporatism, in that trade unions and employers' groups have had a say in the elaboration of policy.

Fascist corporatism differed in that it is predicated upon destruction or purging of existing associations, for it assumed that once unpatriotic left-wing influences had been eliminated, the natural patriotism of all classes would re-emerge, thus allowing them to collaborate in the right spirit. Corporatism supposedly protected workers from the exploitation to which they are subject in a free market—in which wages are at the mercy of the capitalist's whim. Class conflict would give way to national harmony.

Other questions were open. What role should the state and/or party play in the corporations? Should they have the power to fix prices and wages? What concessions would capitalists make to entice workers back into the national community? How much autonomy should be accorded to fascist workers' unions? Those who wanted the greatest degree of freedom for workers' unions were often known as 'syndicalists'.

In Italy, the heirs of the INA emphasized state control over corporatist bodies, while technocrats around Giuseppe Bottai wanted more power for managers and engineers, and Fascist trade unionists wanted autonomy for workers' unions. Business generally opposed any form of compulsory corporatism as a constraint upon free enterprise—whilst asking the state to provide legal backing for their own price-fixing cartels! In other words, the power struggles of democratic society continued in the Fascist regime, but thanks to the suppression of the left, the workers were even more disadvantaged than usual (see Figure 11).

In 1925, Fascist unions launched strikes in the metal-working industry in a bid to impose their views. Under the Palazzo Vidoni agreement of October 1925, they obtained a monopoly of workers' representation—to the annoyance of business, which saw Fascist

11. A Spanish worker salutes a parade of the Falange in 1937. The Falange prided themselves on the originality of their programme for the workers

unions as nearly as dangerous as socialist bodies. Yet the unions failed to obtain parity with employers' organizations in the corporatist structure, which the state began to inaugurate at the same time. Business won out because strikes were banned and unions were declared to be agents of the state. Business still feared Bottai's advocacy of power for managers and engineers, yet it cannot be denied that capitalists scored a victory.

The Nazi Party also included a strong trade union wing in the form of its factory cell organization, the NSBO. After 1933, NSBO leaders, thinking their day had dawned, threatened bosses with concentration camps if they didn't pay higher wages. Hitler's suppression of the SA in 1934, partly as a result of conservative pressure, was a heavy blow to workers' groups. Already, the NSBO had been incorporated into the corporatist German Labour Front (DAF). In practice, the destruction of left-wing unions and the banning of strikes, together with endorsement of management's right to manage, ensured that German workers lacked collective representation. Yet the Labour Front did provide jobs and advancement for ideologically committed workers, and it became one of the 'fiefdoms' that undermined the old state hierarchy. The Nazis also retained much of Weimar's welfare system and set up a 'Strength Through Joy' movement to regulate workers' leisure. Both organizations were harnessed to racial and eugenic projects. Welfare served the goal of incorporating all classes into an ethnically pure, militarily strong national community.

The fortunes of peasants and artisans in the two fascist regimes were similar to those of workers. Both Fascists and Nazis had advocated restoration of the position of these classes, yet achieved little in practice. The Italian Fascists' promise of land to the smallholding peasantry was largely unfulfilled. Mussolini's campaign to prevent rural depopulation didn't prevent the population of Rome from doubling during the life of the regime. In Germany, Nazi shopkeeper and artisan organizations were given little freedom of action. Promises to suppress department stores were broken, while big rather than small business benefited from the confiscation of Jewish property. The Nazis helped indebted peasants, yet did not do enough to prevent the numerical decline of the rural population.

Fascist unions and syndicalism were not just devices to fool the lower classes, for many fascists were prepared to go to great lengths to realize their goals. Fascist unionism failed because it lacked the power to achieve its ends. The national interest was never strong enough to 'discipline' savage capitalism, especially as capitalists and many fascists believed a strong capitalism to be in the national interest. Both regimes saw big business as essential to war production, and gave such firms priority in the allocation of raw materials and labour.

The position of the workers was not, however, defined simply by their subservience to capitalism (any more than the position of the bourgeois women who staffed fascist welfare organizations was defined only by subservience to men). Research into 'everyday life' under Nazism suggests that whilst older workers often remained hostile to Nazism, younger workers redirected aspirations for a better society, previously expressed by socialist parties, into Nazism. The Social Democrats, after all, had never been immune to nationalism. Once socialism had proved its ineffectiveness in 1932–3, the Nazis seem to have won over some of their voters. Historians have suggested that working-class soldiers regarded participation in the regime's race crimes in the East as an extension of the 'high-quality German work' they had once proudly done in the factories. In effect, in return for abandoning class solidarities, workers were offered minor parts in a racist colonial project and a share of the benefits of foreign conquest. In Germany, in defiance of the values of the international labour movement, workers lorded it over millions of slave labourers.

Business and fascism

Does all that mean that fascism was 'ultimately' a business ideology, as some Marxists have suggested?

Yes, it was, in the sense that business interests in both Germany and Italy joined fascist movements. And once Fascism and Nazism had won power, big business largely supported them and viewed the destruction of the labour movement positively.

The answer to this question is also, no, it was not. While capitalists in many countries were happy to use fascists to fight the left, relatively few capitalists actually wanted to install fascist regimes. In Italy, right up to the Fascist seizure of power, business preferred either the INA or Giolitti's liberalism. In Germany, big business did much to undermine democracy, yet the majority of business people would have preferred a conservative dictatorship, with Nazi support, to a Hitler government. Agrarian interests were more active than big business in the negotiations that finally brought Hitler to power.

Again, the answer is no, in the sense that describing fascism as a capitalist regime is not saying much, for big business has demonstrated an enormous ability to adapt to regimes to which it is opposed in principle. Neither is it likely that only recourse to fascism could have saved German or Italian capitalism in the interwar period (whatever it meant to 'save' capitalism). Some business people joined fascist movements in the *belief* that there was no alternative, but their belief was erroneous. Indeed, in the particular historical circumstances of Italy in 1922 and Germany in 1933 most business people didn't see things this way.

In fact, fascism did not defend property absolutely, any more than it did the family. Fascist regimes regulated business in the national interest, especially in pursuit of war, whilst

12. Nazism and private property: the Aryanization of a Jewish owned shop in Frankfurt am Main c.1938. The sign reads Stamm & Bassermann formerly Gummi Weil

destroying its capability of intervening as a body in political decision-making. The Italian regime built a strong nationalized sector in the 1930s. True, private industry continued to prosper, but the strength of the public sector helped to alienate conservatives from the Fascist regime during the war. Most strikingly, the Nazi regime expropriated Jewish property (see Figure 12). In Germany, Jewish business was a small proportion of the total, but in Eastern Europe, especially in Hungary, fascists threatened to expropriate huge sections of capitalism, on the grounds that it was ethnically alien, and they were bitterly opposed by conservatives for that reason.

Marxists might object that many people, including business people, joined fascist movements out of hostility to Marxism, and that fascist ultranationalism represented an attempt to undermine workers' class loyalties. That's all true. Yet it's quite another thing to argue that fascism was *ultimately* a means of defending capitalism. The ideas on which fascists drew contained a plethora of other motivations, conceptions, and ideas, from which the question of capitalism was never absent, yet never the only priority.

Chapter 10
Fascism and us

The legacy of fascism

One way to explore the legacy of fascism is to enter the debate about whether it was a futile attempt to restore 'traditional' society, or helped, perhaps inadvertently, to bring into being the 'modern' world. Partisans of the former view could point to the support of so-called 'antimodern classes' for fascism—artisans, peasants, and aristocratic landowners. Some fascist policies were plausibly antimodern—the return to the land, restriction of city growth, and idealization of the peasantry. Codreanu's fondness for peasant costume expressed Romanian fascism's idealization of the peasantry. Other evidence suggests that fascism was 'modern': the worship of military technology, favouritism towards big business in the distribution of military contracts, mass mobilization, the involvement of women in fascist movements, the promotion of commercialized leisure and sport, and so on.

Evidence can be piled on either side without resolving the question (unless one claims that the evidence that doesn't fit is 'secondary', or a 'means to a more fundamental end'). In fact, we encounter once again the problem of definition—we can't agree what modern is, and so the answer to the question depends on whichever definition we use. In practice, it is hard to avoid judging fascism's modernity in terms of what one personally happens to regard as 'progressive'.

In 1985, Martin Broszat's plea for 'historicization' of scholarly approaches to Nazi Germany illustrated the dangers of unreflecting use of the modernization concept. Historians, he said, should ask more sophisticated, properly historical questions of Nazism rather than simply condemning it morally. Unfortunately, this sensible suggestion was obscured by his conviction that one could achieve that end by examining Nazism's role in promoting or restraining tendencies towards modernization in German society. Introducing the term 'modernization' dragged assumptions about the 'normal' and 'desirable' course of history into the debate. Broszat's argument that the welfare policies of the Nazi Labour Front paved the way for the social policies of modern Germany permitted critics to accuse him of presenting Nazism in a positive light. With some justice, these critics argued that he had artificially isolated the modernization process from other aspects of Nazism, and therefore neglected the racist nature of Nazi welfare policy. Equally problematically, other historians argued that the German Labour Front intended to construct a more 'modern' society in which individual merit mattered more than group membership in determining an individual's social status, but they forgot that in Nazi Germany advancement was restricted by class, gender and race. For instance, working-class cruise passengers resented the privileges of wealthier travellers. Moreover, the Nazis promoted foreign tourism to reveal 'racial inferiority' of destination countries. Of course, there were no Jews among the passengers.

The question of continuity is complex and depends on perspective. Fascist welfare policy was shaped by ultranationalism, political discrimination, and racism. It differed significantly from that of liberal democracies, which generally espouse universal principles and endorse the rights of all individuals to equal treatment. Yet the discriminatory tendencies of fascist social policies are not entirely absent from modern systems, and that might provide fertile ground for the explicit racism of the contemporary far right.

Given the difficulty of determining what is 'modern', a better approach might be to examine how fascists *perceived* and *used* the terms modern and traditional (and even whether they thought in these terms at all). Just as there were many views of what national or class interests meant, there were different views of modernity. What did 'modern' and 'traditional' mean to fascists themselves?

Fascists drew upon Social Darwinism and its French alternative, Lamarckianism, collective psychology, social biology, the science of crowds, and studies of myths. Linking all of these ideas were allegedly scientific assumptions about national characters and/or races. This 'science' was married to the conviction that the nation must be internally strong and homogeneous, if it was to overcome the unavoidable tendency to decadence and survive in the life-and-death international struggle. Here fascists' ideas were shaped by artistic modernism, which perceived the world as a dark, threatening place in which nothing was permanent, which nonetheless might be made sense of and even tamed through the special techniques of the artist.

Many fascists saw this project as modern, but others saw it as a return to tradition, and still others as a reconciliation of tradition and modernity. Beyond that we cannot go. Fascism is a contradictory set of interrelated and contested ideologies and practices that cannot easily be categorized in terms of binary opposites such as tradition and modernity or radical and reactionary.

Fascism and antifascism

That brings me back to the point that I raised at the beginning of the book. If we can't define fascism, how can we identify it and oppose it? If we can't expose a party as fascist, do we let it off the hook?

To begin with, we must not confuse morality with academic research. Moral positions can't be deduced from the study of the past. Scholars can depict the actions of fascism as gruesomely as they wish—alas, they will be seen as *crimes* only if the reader shares the moral perspective of the writer. Anyway, the question of whether or not the modern far right's stance is 'fascist' has no bearing on the moral acceptability of its proposals. For instance, would the expulsion of non-whites from a country be more acceptable if it was the work of a non-fascist government? To reduce the far right to its similarities with fascism carries the risk of obscuring what is new about it and of diverting attention from the possibility that fascists may not be alone in advocating or practicing policies that others would regard as morally wrong.

Another major problem with the definitional obsession is that it forces scholars to take sides in the questions that agitate protagonists—that is, to answer the question of who the true fascists are or were—and thus to provide spurious justification for one side in those disputes. Often, activists or journalists consult academics on the 'definition of a political ideology', in the hope of getting scientific, objective backing for their own views. And yet academics are no better qualified than anyone else is to decide who the real fascists were. They can only explain the different ways that protagonists used the term, classified people, the use they made of those classifications in daily struggles, and what the consequences were. Thanks to their training, academics can justifiably claim to have a special ability in that field, but they have no monopoly on the question of who most truly represents fascism.

As the political sociologist Annie Collovald explains, the FN's adoption of the 'national-populist' label underlines the dangers. This category was not invented by the FN, but by a group of political scientists who occupy a strategic position in the French university establishment, close to governing circles. These academics are committed to the presidential Fifth Republic, which they believe finally satisfies the nation's desire to reconcile democracy with strong government by competent people (such as themselves). They reject the idea that fascism ever existed in mainstream politics in France, for doing so might taint with fascism their own preference for strong government. They therefore depict the FN as a temporary 'national-populist' protest on the part of marginal ill-educated people, who seek simple answers for their difficulties in the age of globalization. Besides betraying a certain contempt for ordinary people, this interpretation plays into the hands of the highly educated professional politicians who actually lead the FN. It permits the FN to assert academic support for its difference from fascism and for its claim to represent the voiceless. It's as if racism is acceptable as long as it isn't fascist. It would be just as problematic though to label the FN as fascist. It's potentially a way of discrediting the party, but since FN sympathizers don't usually see themselves as fascist, one runs the risk of reinforcing their conviction that the movement represents honest people who are contemptuously dismissed by the elite.

Doubtless, those who regard academics' refusal to pronounce as dereliction of duty will not be mollified. Didn't academics use neutrality to claim that the spread of fascism did not concern them? That's undeniably true. However, I would wish to maintain that the approach to fascism that I have outlined in this book does not represent an abdication of moral responsibility. The key point is that academics should not make exaggerated claims for their knowledge, but they must defend the principles on which free and rigorous enquiry depends.

In fact, in the age of fascism, it was precisely the conviction of many academics that 'scientific' methods provided them with special knowledge of what was *morally* good that permitted them to intervene in other people's lives without their consent. The belief that medical science had resolved the question of who should live and die for the good of the nation permitted the involvement of doctors in the Holocaust. Likewise, Italian Fascists believed that since the development of the nation-state was a scientific fact, its preservation ought to be the object of state policy. In reality, the idea that nations have 'characters', or that racial origin determines political behaviour, is mere prejudice which crumbles away under the most limited scrutiny. The science of fascists is little more than bigotry erected into principle.

Although one cannot afford to be complacent, contemporary academics do not usually assume that history is regulated by scientific laws, and still less that knowledge of these laws provides a moral standard. They subject their own assumptions, and those of their colleagues, to systematic criticism, and they try, if not always successfully, to uncover unacknowledged prejudices in their work. A proper scholarly method is intrinsically antifascist, in that it treats sceptically what fascists regard as beyond criticism. Academic enquiry accepts that its insights depend on perspective, that other perspectives will be possible, and that their answers will always be superseded. This neccessary mutual criticism can only happen in a democratic environment.

Notwithstanding, one might still object that this view of academic research promotes 'ivory tower' detachment, and legitimates complacent pursuit of irrelevant intellectual problems while the world collapses. One answer is that we might expect academics to stand up for the values of academic research and promote them as a key part of democracy. Also, it's quite legitimate to study fascism in order to discover which means have been most effective in combating it and what might help fight fascism in the future. Nevertheless, caution is required, for the history of fascism alone cannot provide antifascist strategies. Because fascism is so hard to pin down, no single method could be universally effective against it. Banning fascist organizations sometimes works, sometimes it doesn't. There's no telling whether prosecutions for racist propaganda will represent a deterrent or promote sympathy for people who exercise the right of 'free speech' (but who infringe the rule that freedom is constrained by the harm that one might do to others). Sometimes efforts to appease racism in the electorate have deprived fascists of support; in other cases they have legitimated fascism. Clearly, potential supporters of fascism must be offered a better and more humane alternative means of solving their problems. Yet no rule dictates what this alternative must be.

So are we letting the modern far right off the hook by avoiding the question of fascism? Ultimately, responses to fascism depend not upon scholarly assessments of what has happened in the past or on categorization. We cannot oppose the far right by defining it as fascist—however many similarities there undoubtedly are. We must focus rather on the dangers that it represents in the present, and indeed on the recognition that non-fascist movements, including groups that play by democratic rules can also threaten decent values. The question of values is one for society as a whole, not just for academics.

References

Arendt, Hannah, *The Origins of Totalitarianism* (Harcourt, Brace & Co., 1951)

Bauerkämper, Arnd, 'Transnational Fascism: Cross-Border Relations Between Regimes and Movements in Europe, 1922–1939', *East Central Europe* 37, no. 2–3 (2010):79–95

Blinkhorn, Martin, *Fascism and the Right in Europe 1919–1945* (Longman, 2000)

Bosworth, R. J. B., *The Italian Dictatorship: Problems and Perspectives in the Interpretation of Mussolini and Fascism* (Arnold, 1998)

Bosworth, R. J. B., Mussolini (Arnold, 2002)

Bosworth, R. J. B. (ed.), *The Oxford Handbook of Fascism* (Oxford University Press, 2009)

Burleigh, Michael and Wolfgang Wippermann, *The Racial State, Germany 1933–1945* (Cambridge University Press, 1993)

Burleigh, Michael, *The Third Reich: A New History* (Macmillan, 2000)

Collovald, Annie, 'Le "national-populisme" ou le fascisme disparu. Les historiens du «temps présent» et la question du déloyalisme politique contemporain', in Michel Dobry (ed.), *Le mythe de l'allergie française au fascisme* (Albin Michel, 2003)

De Grand, Alexander, *Italian Fascism: Its Origins and Development* (University of Nebraska Press, 1982)

De Grazia, Victoria, *How Fascism Ruled Italian Women: Italy, 1922–1945* (University of California Press, 1992)

Dobratz, Betty E. and Stephanie L. Shanks-Meile, *'White Power, White Pride': The White Separatist Movement in the United States* (Johns Hopkins University Press, 2000)

Dobry, Michel, 'On an Imaginary Fascism', in *France in the Era of Fascism: Essays on the French Authoritarian Right*, edited by Brian Jenkins (Berghahn Books, 2007), 129–150

Durham, Martin, *The Christian Right, the Far Right and the Boundaries of American Conservatism* (Manchester University Press, 2000)

Eatwell, Roger, *Fascism: A History* (Vintage, 1996)

Eley, Geoff, *Nazism as Fascism* (Routledge, 2013)

Evans, Richard J., *The Coming of the Third Reich* (Allen Lane, 2003)

Evans, Richard J., *The Third Reich in Power, 1933–1939* (Penguin, 2012)

Fritzsche, Peter, *Germans into Nazis* (Harvard University Press, 1998)

Griffin, Roger, *The Nature of Fascism* (Pinter, 1991)

Griffin, Roger, *Modernism and Fascism: The Sense of a Beginning Under Mussolini and Hitler* (Palgrave, 2007)

Hancock, Eleanor, "Only the real, the true, the masculine held its value": Ernst Röhm, masculinity, and male homosexuality', *Journal of the History of Sexuality*, 8:4 (1998), 616–641

Iordachi, Constantin, *Comparative Fascist Studies: New Perspectives* (Routledge, 2010)

Laclau, Ernsto, 'Fascism and Ideology' and 'Toward a Theory of Populism', in *Politics and Ideology in Marxist Theory: Capitalism, Fascism, Populism* (NLB, 1977)

Kershaw, Ian, *Hitler*, 2 vols (Allen Lane, 1998–2000)

Koonz, Claudia, *Mothers in the Fatherland: Women, the Family, and Nazi Politics* (St Martin's Press, 1987)

Mosse, George L., *The Fascist Revolution: Towards a General Theory of Fascism* (Howard Fertig, 1999)

Passmore, Kevin (ed.), *Women, Gender and Fascism in Europe, 1919–1945* (Manchester University Press, 2002)

Paxton, Robert O., *The Anatomy of Fascism* (Penguin, 2004)

Payne, Stanley, *A History of Fascism 1919–1945* (University of Wisconsin Press, 1995)

Quine, Maria Sophia, *Population Politics in Twentieth-Century Europe* (Routledge, 1996)

Reichardt, Sven, *Faschistische Kampfbünde: Gewalt und Gemeinschaft im italienischen Squadrismus und in der deutschen SA* (Böhlau, 2002)

Index

Fascism

NEOLIBERALISM
A Very Short Introduction
Manfred B. Steger & Ravi K. Roy

Anchored in the principles of the free-market economics,
'neoliberalism' has been associated with such different political
leaders as Ronald Reagan, Margaret Thatcher, Bill Clinton,
Tony Blair, Augusto Pinochet, and Junichiro Koizumi. So is
neoliberalism doomed or will it regain its former glory? Will
reform-minded G-20 leaders embark on a genuine new course or
try to claw their way back to the neoliberal glory days of the
Roaring Nineties? Is there a viable alternative to neoliberalism?
Exploring the origins, core claims, and considerable variations
of neoliberalism, this Very Short Introduction offers a concise
and accessible introduction to one of the most debated 'isms'
of our time.

'This book is a timely and relevant contribution to this urgent
contemporary topic.'

I. K. Gujral, Former Prime Minister of India

ANTISEMITISM
A Very Short Introduction
Steven Beller

Antisemitism - a prejudice against or hatred of Jews - has been a chillingly persistent presence throughout the last millennium, culminating in the dark apogee of the Holocaust. This *Very Short Introduction* examines and untangles the various strands of antisemitism seen throughout history, from medieval religious conflict to 'new' antisemitism in the 21st century. Steven Beller reveals how the phenomenon grew as a political and ideological movement in the 19th century, how it reached it its dark apogee in the worst genocide in modern history - the Holocaust - and how antisemitism still persists around the world today.

www.oup.com/vsi

PROGRESSIVISM
A Very Short Introduction
Walter Nugent

This very timely *Very Short Introduction* offers an engaging overview of progressivism in America--its origins, guiding principles, major leaders and major accomplishments. A many-sided reform movement that lasted from the late 1890s until the early 1920s, progressivism emerged as a response to the excesses of the Gilded Age, an era that plunged working Americans into poverty while a new class of ostentatious millionaires built huge mansions and flaunted their wealth. Progressives fought for worker's compensation, child labour laws, minimum wage and maximum hours legislation; they enacted anti-trust laws, instituted the graduated income tax, won women the right to vote, and laid the groundwork for Roosevelt's New Deal.

www.oup.com/vsi

POLITICS
A Very Short Introduction
Kenneth Minogue

In this provocative but balanced essay, Kenneth
Minogue discusses the development of politics from the
ancient world to the twentieth century. He prompts us to
consider why political systems evolve, how politics offers
both power and order in our society, whether democracy
is always a good thing, and what future politics may
have in the twenty-first century.

> 'This is a fascinating book which sketches, in a very short
> space, one view of the nature of politics ... the reader is
> challenged, provoked and stimulated by Minogue's
> trenchant views.'
> **Ian Davies, *Talking Politics***

> 'a dazzling but unpretentious display of great scholarship
> and humane reflection'
> **Neil O'Sullivan, University of Hull**

www.oup.co.uk/vsi/politics

ONLINE CATALOGUE
A Very Short Introduction

Our online catalogue is designed to make it easy to find your ideal Very Short Introduction. View the entire collection by subject area, watch author videos, read sample chapters, and download reading guides.

SOCIAL MEDIA
Very Short Introduction

Join our community
www.oup.com/vsi

- Join us online at the official Very Short Introductions **Facebook** page.
- Access the thoughts and musings of our authors with our online **blog**.
- Sign up for our monthly **e-newsletter** to receive information on all new titles publishing that month.
- Browse the full range of Very Short Introductions online.
- Read **extracts** from the Introductions for free.
- Visit our library of **Reading Guides**. These guides, written by our expert authors will help you to question again, why you think what you think.
- If you are a teacher or lecturer you can order inspection copies quickly and simply via our website.